Púlpito

Púlpito

An Introduction to Hispanic Preaching

Justo L. González

and

Pablo A. Jiménez

Abingdon Press
Nashville

PÚLPITO
AN INTRODUCTION TO HISPANIC PREACHING

Library of Congress Cataloging-in-Publication Data

Púlpito : an introduction to Hispanic preaching / [edited by] Justo L. González and Pablo A. Jiménez.
      p. cm.
    Includes bibliographical references.
    ISBN 0-687-08850-X (binding: pbk. : alk. paper)
    1. Hispanic American preaching.   2. Hispanic American Protestants—Religious life.   I. González, Justo L.   II. Jiménez, Pablo A.
    BV4208.U6P85 2005
    2518.0089868073—dc22

                                                                                      2005001744

06 07 08 09 10 11 12 13 14—10 9 8 7 6 5 4 3 2

MANUFACTURED IN THE UNITED STATES OF AMERICA

Justo dedicates this book to his wife, Catherine,
with love.

Pablo dedicates this book to the Reverend Durstan McDonald,
former president of the Episcopal Theological Seminary of the
Southwest, and to his former students of homiletics
at that institution.

CONTENTS

Introduction

The Hispanic community is the fastest growing segment of the population in the United States. According to 2004 estimates of the Bureau of the Census, almost 40 million Latinos and Latinas live permanently in the nation. Furthermore, the Bureau estimates that in the next decades the number of Hispanics living in the United States will surpass 50 million. Hispanics have become the largest minority group in the nation, and will soon outnumber the African American population in every region of the United States.

As is true of many other minority communities, Hispanics are deeply religious. While most Anglo-European denominations register a decline in membership, Hispanic congregations are growing constantly. This development transcends geographical and denominational boundaries, as Catholic, mainline Protestant, and Pentecostal churches develop in different parts of the nation.

Parallel to the growth of the Hispanic church, Latino and Latina religious scholars are collaborating in the development of Hispanic theology. The movement, born in the late seventies, is making an important contribution to the American religious scene through its publications and through the many organizations created to foster the theological education of Hispanics.[1]

The Hispanic theological bibliography is also increasing rapidly. There are two theological journals dedicated to Hispanic theology: *Apuntes*, published by the Mexican-American Program at Perkins School of Theology since 1981 and the *Journal for Latino/Hispanic Theology*, published by the Association of Catholic Hispanic Theologians in the United States (ACHTUS) since 1993. There are also an increasing number of publications in both English and Spanish that address a wide spectrum of biblical, theological, and ethical issues from a Hispanic perspective.[2] As expected, the earliest publications focused on the traditional theological fields. Lately, the focus has broadened to include books addressing topics in pastoral theology and ministerial preparation.[3]

However, in contrast to other minority communities, there is still little written in English about homiletics from a Hispanic Protestant perspective. While it is relatively easy to find published articles and books on African American, feminist, or womanist preaching, materials on Hispanic homiletics are scarce. Even a thorough search of the religious indexes will yield only a handful of articles on the subject, most of them in Spanish. In part, this explains why the larger academic homiletic guild seldom addresses the issue of Hispanic preaching in their writings or classrooms. The aim of this book is precisely to offer a comprehensive introduction to Hispanic preaching. In order to achieve such a goal, this introduction seeks to reflect the trademark characteristics of Latino and Latina religiosity and theology. First, the book has been written *en conjunto* (collegially) by authors deeply committed to the Hispanic community. Jiménez wrote the first and third chapters, while González wrote the second and the fourth. Both collaborated in the compilation and edition of the rest of the book. Second, the book blends theory and practice, including in its second part a collection of sermons that exemplifies the principles discussed in the first part. Third, it reflects the ecumenical thrust that characterizes most Hispanic theological endeavors. Finally, even though its focus is the Hispanic community, this study intends to make a contribution to the larger religious academic community and to the church as a whole.

The book is divided into two parts. The first part, titled "Around the *Púlpito*," contains four chapters that discuss homiletic theory from a Hispanic perspective. Chapter 1 describes the development of contemporary Hispanic homiolectics, offering a brief historical survey of the development of Hispanic preaching. Chapter 2 discusses the impact of several theological and cultural issues on the *púlpito*. Chapter 3 expounds on Hispanic hermeneutics, using as backdrop the story of Mary and Martha (Luke 10:38-42). The fourth and last chapter of this first part explores sermon delivery from a Hispanic perspective.

The second part is made up of ten sermons: four by the authors plus six by distinguished Latino and Latina preachers with extensive pastoral experience. Minerva Carcaño preaches about the plight of poor children. Elizabeth Conde-Frazier develops a sermon about worship. Virgilio Elizondo brings a dialogical sermon for Good Friday. Justo L. González contributes two sermons on different parables of Jesus. Pablo A. Jiménez presents a sermon on a Pauline christological hymn and a bilingual sermon on the parable of the pearl. Joel Martínez calls us to renew our baptismal vows. Yolanda Pupo-Ortiz preaches about spirituality. Roberto A. Rivera offers us a sermon on Abraham's attempted sacrifice of Isaac, his son. We offer these comments and reflections in the hope of informing the larger homiletic academic community about the "hidden history" of homiletics in the Hispanic Protestant community. We hope to advance the discussion of the subject, thus inviting all readers to the study and practice of the art of Christian preaching.

Notes

1. Some of these organizations are: the Academy of Catholic Hispanic Theologians in the United States (ACHTUS); the Hispanic Summer Program (HSP); the Asociación para la Educación Teológica Hispana (AETH); the *Asociación de Ministerios Evangélicos Nacionales* (AMEN); and the Hispanic Theological Initiative (HTI).

2. See, for example, Paul Barton and David Maldonado, Jr., *Hispanic Christianity Within Mainline Protestant Traditions: A Bibliography* (Decatur, Ga.: AETH Books, 1998). Also, the *Journal of Hispanic/Latino Theology* publishes an annual review of the Latino publications of the year.

3. See, for example, Justo L. González, editor, *¡Alabadle! Hispanic Christian Worship* (Nashville: Abingdon Press, 1996).

PART I

Around the Púlpito

Hispanic Homiletic Theory

CHAPTER ONE

Building the Púlpito

Pablo A. Jiménez

In order to understand the development of Hispanic Protestant homiletic theory in the United States, one has to analyze how such theory arrived at the Latin American *púlpito*. We also need to research how it was interpreted and who reinterpreted it. Only then will we be able to understand how homiletic theory is being modified and recast by contemporary Hispanic-American scholars.

This brief historical survey is divided into three broad sections. The first describes the earliest Protestant manuals on homiletics translated into Spanish and used widely in Latin America and the Caribbean. The second reviews the most influential homiletic manuals written by Latin Americans. The third explores how contemporary Hispanic-American scholars are reinterpreting the inherited homiletic theory in the light of their own Latino subculture.

Before going any further, I must qualify my comments in two different ways. First, in this survey I refer mostly to manuals on homiletics that have been distributed widely in Latin America and the United States. I am aware that this decision excludes other important homiletic materials, such as regional publications, collections of sermons, and articles published in theological journals and religious magazines. Second, like any other historical periodization, this survey is selective (some may say arbitrary). It could be easily modified, improved, or even challenged. Once again, the aim is to open—not to close—discussion and research of these issues.[1]

First Stage: Transculturation

Protestant homiletic theory arrived in Latin America early in the 1900s, hand in hand with the missionaries. Up to that point, Protestantism had a rather long and tormented history in Latin America.[2] The first Protestants arrived in South America and the Caribbean in the sixteenth century, at the time of the Spanish Conquest. However, most of them were either banished or exterminated by the Spanish Inquisition. European immigrants established the first Protestant congregations in Latin America early in the nineteenth century. We can divide these congregations into two categories.[3] The earliest were the "transplanted" congregations that exclusively served British merchants and their families. These were established through agreements between the British and Spanish crowns. Their existence testifies to the enormous influence in Latin America of trade with Great Britain. These congregations were not allowed to proselytize Spanish subjects. Ethnic groups invited to immigrate to Latin America by the new national governments established the second type of immigrant congregations. The aim of such "grafted" congregations was the pastoral care of the immigrant community, keeping proselytism to a minimum. Both categories of ethnic congregations shared a common trait: they "imported" their ministers from their homelands. Hence, immigrant ministers studied homiletics in Europe or in the United States.

The first Protestant missionaries arrived in Latin America in the nineteenth century. These missionaries can be classified in three broad categories: those associated with para-ecclesial organizations (such as the Bible Societies); those belonging to mainline denominations in the United States; and those sponsored by "faith missions."

The "faith missions" were independent missionary groups. They were usually supported by laypersons in Great Britain or the United States, countries that provided most missionaries. The main reason for the emergence of such independent groups was the reluctance of mainline churches to engage in missionary work in Latin America. Unlike Africa and Asia, Latin America was a "Christian continent," evangelized by the Roman Catholic Church. Many missionary organizations associated with mainline churches did not see Latin America as a legitimate field of mission. Therefore, both the mainline and the independent missionaries to Latin America tended to be more conservative and anti-Catholic that their counterparts in other parts of the globe. The Protestant missionaries who reached Latin America considered the development of new congregations the primary element in the mission of the church. Effective evangelistic preaching was seen as a key tool in church planting and con-

4

gregational growth. Therefore, missionaries promoted the translation into Spanish of well-known manuals of homiletics. They needed such manuals to train lay preachers and candidates to the ministry.

Four of the manuals that circulated in this period deserve special attention. The first three are the Spanish translations of English books: *Lectures to My Students* by Charles H. Spurgeon; *On the Preparation and Delivery of Sermons* by John A. Broadus; and *The Preparation of Biblical Sermons* by Andrew W. Blackwood. The fourth manual, titled *El sermón eficaz* (The Effective Sermon), was originally written in Spanish by James D. Crane.

Discursos a mis estudiantes, by Charles H. Spurgeon[4]

Spurgeon was a British Baptist preacher, known internationally for his sermons and for being the pastor of the largest regular congregation during the Victorian age. An evangelical Calvinist, his many publications form "the largest body of evangelical writings in the English language."[5] Although his manual, published originally in 1875, addresses important points on sermon design, its main thrust is the spiritual formation of the minister. Its Spanish translation was used mainly to mold the character of prospective preachers. For this reason, it was usually employed in tandem with Broadus's treatise.

Tratado sobre la predicación, by John A. Broadus[6]

This has been arguably the most influential manual of homiletics in Latin America. It presents the sermon as a rhetorical piece intended to instruct and persuade.[7] Its detailed sermon design methodology and rationalistic style appealed particularly to well-educated candidates to the ministry. Such preachers found in Broadus's system a method that reminded them of the Spanish *estilística*—techniques for oral and written expression—that they had learned painstakingly at school. Although its English version was originally published in 1870, this manual is still widely used in Latin America, especially at *Institutos* (community-based non-degree-granting theological schools for lay leaders and licensed preachers).

La preparación de sermones bíblicos by Andrew W. Blackwood[8]

Broadus was to homiletic theory as Blackwood was to expository preaching. The work of this Presbyterian minister shaped the way Latin

5

American Protestant preachers designed their biblical sermons. Blackwood's methodology calls for a twofold approach to homiletics.[9] First, it encourages the study of the sermons and publications of outstanding preachers. Second, it pays scrupulous attention to sermon design, since it also sees the sermon as a rhetorical composition. Like Broadus, his methodology appealed mostly to the well educated.

El sermón eficaz, by James D. Crane[10]

Crane was a Baptist missionary who had a long teaching career in Latin America, especially in Argentina. Although his book was written originally in Spanish, it is a rather complicated re-elaboration of Broadus's homiletic theory. For this reason, Crane's and Broadus's manuals have come to be seen as interchangeable in Latin America. Crane also published a simplified version of his homiletic system in the book *Manual para predicadores laicos* (A Manual for Lay Preachers).[11]

Although translations of other books on homiletics—such as Horne's *The Romance of Preaching*—also circulated in Latin America, the aforementioned have been the most influential. They take a similar approach to homiletics: a deductive, neo-classical or rationalistic understanding of sermon design; an Anglo-American worldview; and a "free church" perspective that discourages the use of lectionaries and does little to relate the sermon to the liturgy. Maybe this explains why the same company, *Casa Bautista de Publicaciones*, the Spanish division of the Southern Baptist Publishing House in El Paso, Texas, has published them. A testimony to the endurance of these four manuals and of the homiletic views they hold is that they are still in print.

Second Stage: Inculturation

The homiletic theory described above found fertile ground in Latin America. As mentioned earlier, it appealed particularly to well-educated candidates to the ministry. These preachers developed styles that blended Broadus's deductive homiletic theory with Spanish oratory. The best ones displayed an outstanding level of erudition, extracting illustrations from the best Spanish literature and anecdotes from classical works. In short, these "learned" preachers were truly poets of the pulpit.

However, not all candidates to the ministry had access to sound education. On the contrary, most Latin American preachers barely had the equivalent of a high school education. Therefore, these "popular" preachers, who had little or no access to theological education, developed their own preaching style. Although there are no formal research papers published in this area, elsewhere I have characterized the popular preaching style as an extemporaneous exposition of a biblical passage.[12] The sermon designs privileged by such style are the narrative sermon, the "reference/concordance" sermon (where the preacher quotes a string of biblical verses as proof texts), and the *testimonio* (where the preacher narrates and interprets theologically an episode of her or his own life).

The contrast between learned and popular Latin American preaching was stark and their relation uneasy. On the one hand, some popular preachers despised the learned style, describing it as a convoluted discourse devoid of the power of the Holy Spirit. On the other hand, some other popular preachers sought to emulate the models presnted by learned preachers. In all fairness, we must recognize that the sermons of the most outstanding Latin American preachers were truly literary jewels.

Not surprisingly, these learned preachers became the first Latin American scholars in the field of homiletics. They published their sermons in theological journals such as *Revista de Homilética*, *El Predicador Evangélico*, *La Nueva Democracia* and *Puerto Rico Evangélico*, among others. In time, they also published books that compiled illustrations, homiletic outlines, and sermons. As expected, learned preachers also became the first Latin American professors of homiletics. Some of them, such as Alberto Rembao,[13] trained scores of seminarians in several countries, thus spinning informal "schools." Others, like Angel Archilla Cabrera[14] and Juan Crisóstomo Varetto,[15] traveled throughout Latin America preaching in "crusades" that followed the model of the American revival and holding public debates with Catholic priests. These learned revivalists became living models for Latin American Protestant preaching. Once again, I will highlight only four of the manuals on homiletics published in this period: *El arte cristiano de la predicación* (The Christian Art of Preaching) by Angel Mergal; *Comunicación por medio de la predicación* (Communication Through Preaching) by Orlando E. Costas; *Predicación y misión: Una perspectiva pastoral* (Preaching and Mission: A Pastoral Perspective) by Osvaldo Mottesi; and *Teoría y práctica de la predicación* (Theory and Practice of Preaching) by Cecilio Arrastía.

El arte cristiano de la preedicación, by Angel Mergal[16]

Mergal had a long tenure as professor in the Evangelical Seminary of Puerto Rico (ESPR). He was considered a genius, teaching biblical languages, German, homiletics, and pastoral counseling, among other courses. His handbook is divided into two parts. The first affirms that preaching is an art, expounding on the aesthetic qualities of the discipline. This section is informed by the philosophy of Suzanne K. Langer.[17] The second and shorter section addresses sermon design. Although the latter part pales in comparison to the first, this beautiful book may well be the best manual on homiletics ever written in Latin America.

Comunicación por medio de la predicación by Orlando E. Costas[18]

The renowned Puerto Rican missiologist was also a student and a teacher of homiletics. Costas wrote this comprehensive handbook on preaching while teaching at the then Latin American Biblical Seminary (now University) in San José, Costa Rica. Although in many ways Costas follows on Broadus's steps, his book made twso important contributions to Latin American homiletics. First, Costas brought a new theological perspective to the field. Although he defined himself as an evangelical, even at this early stage of his career his progressive theology was in dialogue with neo-orthodox and even Catholic perspectives. Second, he presents preaching as a communication process, taking into consideration insights from speech and mass communication.[19] An interesting note is the clear influence of the works of Lloyd M. Perry on Costas's methodology.[20]

Predicación y misión: Una perspectiva pastoral by Osvaldo Mottesi[21]

This excellent Argentinean preacher studied homiletics under James D. Crane in the *Instituto Bautista de Buenos Aires*. An Emory graduate, he also taught homiletics at the Latin American Biblical Seminary in Costa Rica before beginning his long tenure at Northern Baptist Theological Seminary. As expected, his manual follows the rhetorical emphasis taught by Crane. Nonetheless, this work makes a decisive contribution to the field. Mottesi teaches homiletics against the backdrop provided by the radical evangelical missiology developed in Latin America during the late seventies and eighties.[22] His methodology is thus contextual and pastoral. Therefore, the book has a decided Latin American flavor.

Teoría y práctica de la predicación, by Cecilio Arrastía[23]

For decades Cecilio Arrastía was considered the best Latin American preacher and the foremost Hispanic homiletician.[24] This Cuban American was renowned for his learned and powerful preaching. He did it all: preaching international crusades, publishing collections of sermons, writing on homiletic theory, and teaching homiletics in many formal and informal settings, including ESPR and McCormick Theological Seminary. Although he published many technical articles on homiletics in theological journals,[25] his first books where collections of sermons.[26] Since the seventies his students clamored for a textbook written by the "master homiletician." Yet, Arrastía did not publish his textbook until after his retirement. Paradoxically, the junior contemporary of Mergal and the mentor of Costas and Mottesi[27] was the last one to publish his homiletics survey.

Arrastía's survey is not a traditional homiletics manual. Although it also sees the sermon as a rhetorical composition, it expounds the author's eclectic methodology. The manual makes four important contributions to Latin American homiletics. First, it explains Arrastía's painstaking sermon design methodology. Second, it offers a detailed explanation of the Christian year and the use of the lectionary, departing from the "free church" emphasis that historically has dominated the discipline in Latin America. Third, it includes a long chapter on the use of literature in preaching, citing hundreds of classic, Spanish, and Latin American works in the bibliography. Finally, he affirms that the local congregation is a "hermeneutic community." This leads him to propose different ways of devising "collegial sermons," where the congregation takes part in the preparation, the evaluation and even the delivery of the sermon.[28]

Significantly, the authors of these four manuals on homiletics are technically Hispanics; two of them are Puerto Ricans—who are U.S. citizens by birth—and the other two are Latin Americans who came to live permanently in the United States. For this reason, their homiletic systems made an impact not only in Latin America, but also within the Hispanic American church.

I must also stress that these books are only a small part of the contribution that these scholars made to Latin and Hispanic American preaching. Their actual preaching in local churches, denominational events, crusades, revivals, and other occasions has been their principal contribution to the Latino church. Thanks to Mergal, Costas, Mottesi, and Arrastía, the model of the learned preacher of the past—the gifted orator who mastered both the Spanish language and theological erudition—still haunts the Hispanic pulpit.

Third Stage: Contextualization

In this section I assess the impact of the aforementioned homiletic theory on the Hispanic American Protestant church.[29] I pay special attention to the way in which Hispanic preachers and theologians are recasting the teachings of Mergal, Costas, Mottesi, and Arrastía.

During the last three decades Hispanic leaders, theologians, and religious scholars have been developing a distinct theological movement. Hispanic theology is a contextual or "political" theology, done from a Latino and Latina perspective. Its point of departure is Hispanic social location; the reality that the Latino community experiences daily in the United States. Such reality is characterized by the religious experience of the Hispanic community and the marginalization suffered by the Latino people. Hispanic theology also advances a methodology that advocates a praxis of liberation, seeking thus the transformation of the oppressive reality endured daily by the Latino people.

Hispanic theology is transforming the way Latino and Latina scholars approach the different theological disciplines. This will be the focus of the next chapter. It is also transforming the way Hispanics understand and approach biblical hermeneutics, a topic addressed in the third chapter. The focus of the remainder of this chapter is the direct contribution of Hispanic American scholars to homiletics.

Once more, I highlight four manuals on homiletics and hermeneutics published in this period: *Predicación evangélica y teología hispana* (Protestant Preaching and Hispanic Theology) edited by Orlando E. Costas; *Liberation Preaching*, by Justo L. and Catherine G. González; *Lumbrera a nuestro camino* (A Lamp to Our Feet) edited by Pablo A. Jiménez; and *Púlpito cristiano y justicia social* (The Christian Pulpit and Social Justice) edited by Daniel R. Rodríguez-Díaz. Following this is a brief discussion of the contribution of Latinas to the theory and practice of homiletics, particularly of Sandra Mangual-Rodríguez.

Predicación evangélica y teología hispana, edited by Orlando E. Costas[30]

For those who never met Costas, it may seem odd to examine his contribution in two different periods of our historical survey. Those who knew him will not be surprised. Costas's theological thought was in constant development. In the nine years that passed between the publication of his homiletics survey and this collection of essays, Costas became a well-known missiologist and theologian. Never abandoning his theological roots, he came to define himself as an "Evangelical Liberation" theologian.

Costas was a firebrand. Soon after moving back to the United States, he began to organize Hispanic leaders, seminarians, and theologians. His book comprises the papers presented at the first symposium he convened in the States. His goal was to establish a chapter of the Latin American Theological Fraternity in the United States. Although that goal was not accomplished then, the symposium followed a pattern that soon became entrenched in Hispanic circles. The gathering was interdenominational, intergenerational, bicultural, and bilingual. It assumed a broad interpretation of theological education, drawing together local pastors, representatives from *Institutos* and Bible colleges, seminarians, and seminary professors. It called Latinos and Latinas to do theology side by side. Hispanics call this methodology *Teología en conjunto* (collegial theology). All the books studied in this section represent such *Teología en conjunto* in one way or another.

Costas's book does not conceive the sermon as a rhetorical composition. As a matter of fact, it does not address the traditional homiletic loci, such as the invention, the design, or the delivery of the sermon. This is a theological book. The first part traces biblical perspectives on the concept "the word of God." The second part explores the relation between homiletics and Hispanic culture and identity. This is a truly dialogical section, where the main exposition of each topic is followed by comments from two other participants. Some of those responses are in English. The third part addresses the interdisciplinary character of preaching, probing the relationships among preaching, spirituality, education, counseling, and comunication. This book made a decisive contribution to Latino and Latina homiletics.

Liberation Preaching: The Pulpit and the Oppressed by Justo L. and Catherine G. González[31]

Technically, this is not a book on Hispanic preaching. Its scope is much broader, analyzing the contribution to homiletics of a wide array of contextual, political, and liberation theologies. Nonetheless, Justo's references to his experience as a Latino offer important perspectives on Hispanic preaching. This writing is relevant to Hispanic theology for several reasons. First, it calls the preacher to read the Bible from the standpoint of the powerless, reexamining the dominant biblical interpretations through a "hermeneutics of suspicion." For Hispanics, this means to interpret Scripture from our "place," a social location of powerlessness, oppression, poverty, racism, and discrimination. Second, it empowers the preacher to ask "political questions" from the text: Who are the powerful? Who are the powerless? What are the sources of social and political power? Is power used in an ethical manner? This leads the preacher to fashion contextual sermons that are relevant to the reality of the Latino people. Finally, and perhaps more important, it affirms the validity of the Hispanic experience as a source of theology.

Lumbrera a nuestro camino, edited by Pablo A. Jiménez[32]

This book comprises papers presented at the First *Encuentro* of Hispanic Biblical Scholars, a symposium organized by the *Asociación para la Educación Teológica Hispana* (AETH). Although the thrust of the book is biblical scholarship, it addresses homiletic concerns in every chapter. Once again, the book reflects the collegial methodology followed in the symposium, offering brief critical responses to the main presentations. The initial chapters explore cutting-edge issues in the study of the Hebrew Bible and the New Testament. The middle ones outline the history of biblical interpretation. The latter chapters study the relationship between hermeneutics, homiletics, and Christian education. The main characteristic of this manual is precisely its cultural awareness. Written after the publication of seminal works in Latino and Latina theology,[33] its contributors write from a theological perspective that faithfully represents the hopes and wants of the Hispanic *púlpito*.

Predicación evangélica y justicia social, edited by Daniel R. Rodríguez-Díaz[34]

This collaboration of Hispanic American and Mexican authors comprises essays on homiletic theory and sermons. As the title implies, the book emphasizes the relationship between preaching and social issues such as justice, race, gender, and immigration, among others. In a way, the book as a whole is a good example of liberation preaching.

I must also underscore the important contribution of Latinas to Hispanic preaching. It is common to see Hispanic women in the *púlpito*, both in Latin America and in the United States. In part, this is an unlikely by-product of the racism that otherwise tainted missionary endeavors in Latin America and the Caribbean. As missions grew south of the border, missionaries were forced to delegate ministerial duties. Given their initial reticence to entrust pastoral work to locals, male missionaries usually turned to their wives and to single female missionaries. Unwittingly, these women became role models. Church members grew accustomed to female leadership in the local congregation and female presence in the *púlpito*. This led the second and third generations to appoint women as *misioneras* (lay preachers) and *pastoras* (local pastors) even in denominations that traditionally did not ordain women.

A number of women have excelled in the *púlpito* and in the classroom. The pioneers, such as the Reverend "Mama" Leo Rosado in New York City, inspired younger generations of women to embrace the preaching ministry. The younger generations are making an important contribution to the field of homiletics. Many Latinas preach in local congregations, write on homiletics, and teach at *Instituto* and seminary levels.[35] By far, the most important Latina homiletician has been Sandra Mangual-Rodríguez. Dr. Mangual studied homiletics with Arrastía at ESPR and with Costas at Andover-Newton Theological School.[36] She became a seminary professor, training hundreds of Latino and Latina preachers at ESPR and at three different sessions of the Hispanic Summer Program. Her approach to homiletics blended the sound homiletic theory learned from her distinguished teachers with elements of Hispanic, feminist, and *Mujerista* theology.[37]

The Road Ahead

The works described in the latter part of our historical survey point to the emergence of a new way of engaging the *púlpito*.[38] Latinos and Latinas are developing a homiletic theory that is centered on function and content, not on traditional sermon design. If Christian preaching is indeed the theological interpretation of life, the aim of Hispanic preaching must then be the theological interpretation of the Latino and Latina experience. Beyond teaching parishioners the rudiments of the Christian faith, the aim of Hispanic preaching must be helping the Latino community to develop and maintain their cultural identity, even as such identity is modified by the experience of living permanently in the United States. The *púlpito* should also equip the Hispanic community to resist the social manifestations of evil that try to destroy the Latino people through racism, sexism, xenophobia, and classism. In a word, it is our conviction that, through the *púlpito*, God seeks to empower Hispanics to persevere and prevail in their *lucha por la vida,* in their struggle for life.

In order to achieve such a goal, the Hispanic church must follow a two-fold strategy. First, we need continued education programs for the scores of Latino and Latina lay leaders, licensed ministers, and pastoral agents who have little or no formal theological training. Hispanic preachers need the help of Latino and Latina scholars to interpret the challenges raised by their experience of oppression, discrimination, marginalization, otherness, exile, and diaspora. Second, we must foster the development of Latino and Latina scholars duly prepared to analyze and engage the theological issues raised by the Hispanic experience. The goal is to develop "organic intellectuals"; laypeople, pastors, and theologians who can move with ease from the *púlpito*, to the academy, to the community at large, and back to the *púlpito*.

Notes

1. Others have published brief historical overviews on Latin American preaching: *Diccionario de Historia de la Iglesia* (hereafter DHI), edited by Wilton M. Nelson, s.v. "Predicación evangélica en América Latina" by Orlando E. Costas (Miami: Editorial Caribe, 1989), p. 863; *Concise Encyclopedia of Preaching* (hereafter CEP), edited by William M. Willimon and Richard Lischer, "Homiletics and Preaching in Latin America" by John L. Kater (Westminster/John Knox, 1995), pp. 241-43.

2. For an introduction to the history of Protestantism in Latin America see José Míguez Bonino, *Faces of Latin American Protestantism* (Grand Rapids, Mich.: Eerdmans, 1995). For an in-depth study, see Enrique Dussell, *The Church in Latin America, 1492–1992* (Maryknoll: Orbis, 1992).

3. Christian Lalive D'Epinay, building on Weber's distinction between church and sect, describes five types of Protestant groups in Latin America: (1) Churches of "transplanted" immigrants; (2) denominations established by immigrant "grafted" communities; (3) mainline denominations; (4) "sanctification" Protestant sects; and (5) Pentecostal "faith missions." See his article "Toward a

Typology of Latin American Protestantism," *Review of Religious Research* 10 (Fall 1968), pp. 4-11.

4. El Paso: *Casa Bautista de Publicaciones*, 1950.

5. CEP, s.v. "Spurgeon, Charles Haddon" by Craig Skinner, p. 450.

6. El Paso: *Casa Bautista de Publicaciones*, 1925.

7. CEP, s.v. "Broadus, John Albert" by Al Fasol, pp. 45-46; s.v. "Homiletics and Preaching in North America" by Don M. Wardlaw, pp. 245-46; s.v. "Rhetoric" by Craig A. Loscalzo, pp. 411-12.

8. El Paso: *Casa Bautista de Publicaciones*, 1953.

9. CEP, s.v. "Blackwood, Andrew Watterson" by Wayne E. Shaw, pp. 37-38.

10. El Paso: *Casa Bautista de Publicaciones*, 1961.

11. El Paso: *Casa Bautista de Publicaciones*, 1966.

12. Pablo A. Jiménez, editor, *Lumbrera a nuestro camino* (Miami: Editorial Caribe, 1994), pp. 126-29.

13. DHI, s.v. "Rembao, Alberto," by Cecilio Arrastía, p. 902.

14. DHI, s.v. "Archilla Cabrera, Angel" by W. Dayton Roberts, p. 69.

15. DHI, s.v. "Varetto, Juan Crisóstomo" by Arnoldo Canclini Varetto, p. 1051.

16. Mexico: *Casa Unida de Publicaciones*, 1951.

17. Susanne K. Langer, *Philosophy in a New Key: A Study in the Symbolism of Reason* (Cambridge: Harvard University Press, 1957).

18. Miami: Editorial Caribe, 1973.

19. During his tenure in San José, Costas also wrote *Introducción a la Comunicación* (San José: Sebila, 1976).

20. Lloyd M. Perry, *A Manual for Biblical Preaching* (Grand Rapids, Mich.: Baker Book House, 1967); *Biblical Sermon Guide* (Grand Rapids, Mich.: Baker Book House, 1970).

21. Miami: LOGOI, 1989.

22. The Latin American Theological Fraternity, an international group of evangelical theologians, developed a particular approach to missiology during these decades. For a brief description of the organization, see DHI, s.v. "Fraternidad Teológica Latinoamericana" by José Míguez Bonino, p. 465.

23. Miami: Editorial Caribe, 1989.

24. DHI, s.v. "Arrastía Valdes, Cecilio" by Marco Antonio Ramos, pp. 81-82.

25. Plutarco Bonilla, the Costa Rican scholar, compiled and published Arrastía's articles in a special edition of the journal *Pastoralia* 4:9 (1982). They were also published in the book *La predicación, el predicador y la iglesia* (San José: Colección CELEP, 1983).

26. *Jesucristo, Señor del pánico: Antología de Predicaciones* (Mexico: *Casa Unida de Publicaciones*, 1964); *Itinerario de la pasión* (El Paso: *Casa Bautista de Publicaciones*, 1978).

27. Arrastía wrote the prologue to both Costas's and Mottesi's manuals.

28. See his article "La Iglesia como comunidad hermenéutica" in Justo L. González, editor, *Voces: Voices from the Hispanic Church* (Nashville: Abingdon, 1992), pp. 122-27.

29. For an example of the continued development of homiletics in Latin America see Christophe Zenses, *Siervo de la Palabra: Manual de homilética* (Buenos Aires: ISEDET, 1997).

30 San Diego: *Publicaciones de las Américas*, 1982.

31. Nashville: Abingdon Press, 1980. Its revised edition is called *The Liberating Pulpit* (Nashville: Abingdon, 1994).

32. Jiménez, *Lumbrera*.

33. Virgilio Elizondo, *Galilean Journey: The Mexican American Promise* (Maryknoll, N.Y.: Orbis, 1983); Orlando Costas, *Liberating News: A Theology of Contextual Evangelization* (Grand Rapids, Mich.: Eerdmans, 1989); Justo L. González, *Mañana: Christian Theology from a Hispanic Perspective* (Nashville: Abingdon, 1990); Roberto S. Goizueta, editor, *We Are a People! Initiatives in Hispanic Theology* (Minneapolis: Fortress, 1992); Alan Figueroa Deck, editor, *Frontiers of Hispanic American Theology in the United States* (Maryknoll, N.Y.: Orbis Books, 1992); and Ada María Isasi-Díaz, *En La Lucha/In the Struggle: A Hispanic Women's Liberation Theology* (Minneapolis: Fortress, 1993).

34. Mexico: Publicaciones El Faro, 1994.

35. Some of the publications by Latinas are: Loida Martell-Otero, "June 15, 1997: Ordinary Time 11 or Proper 6" and "October 26, 1997: Ordinary Time 30 or Proper 25" in Lucy Rose, editor, *Abingdon's Women Preaching Annual*, Series 1 Year B (Nashville: Abingdon, 1996); and Daisy Machado, "El Cántico de María," *Journal for Preachers* 21:1 (Advent 1997):12-15. Martell-Otero, an American Baptist minister, taught homiletics and hermeneutics in New York Theological Seminary's Hispanic program. Maritza Resto and Inés J. Figueroa, both ordained ministers of the Christian Church (Disciples of Christ) in Puerto Rico, have also taught homiletics at ESPR.

36. See her unpublished D.Min. dissertation, *The Training of Hispanic Protestant Preachers in the United States: An Indigenous Approach to Homiletics* (Newton Centre: Andover Newton Theological School, 1988).

37. For a sample of Mangual's preaching see her sermon "*La danza de la vida en la muerte*" in Ángel Luis Gutiérrez, editor, *Voces del púlpito hispano* (Valley Forge, Pa.: Judson, 1989), pp. 72-78.

38. Two examples of the continuing development of the discipline are Kenneth G. Davis and Jorge L. Presmanes, editors, *Preaching and Culture in Latino Congregations* (Chicago: Liturgical Training Publications, 2000), which presents Catholic perspectives on preaching and liturgy; and Pablo A. Jiménez, *Principios de predicación* (Nashville: Abingdon, 2003), an introductory survey.

CHAPTER TWO

ISSUES AT THE *PÚLPITO*

Justo L. González

Settings and Preachers

As one seeks to analyze Hispanic preaching, there are two major divides that must be taken into account. The first of these has to do with the audience. Hispanic preachers do not speak only to Latino audiences and congregations. Much of our preaching addresses the church at large, and quite often takes place in settings where the vast majority of the congregation is not Hispanic. On the other hand, our day-to-day preaching most often takes place in congregations that are mostly Hispanic. These two very different settings produce two different sorts of preaching—a matter that will be discussed more fully in chapter 4.

The other major divide separates Hispanic preachers who are content with the traditional interpretations of Scripture and of doctrine that were passed on to them, and those others who feel compelled to seek new interpretations by the circumstances in which they and their congregations live. Since the preaching of the former group is quite similar to what most readers of this book will have experienced elsewhere, the rest of this chapter will deal primarily with the manner in which the latter sort of preacher reinterprets Scripture and tradition in the light of the situation of the Latino community.

However, before moving on to the sort of preacher, theological approach to preaching, and the mission of the church that interest us here, it is important to acknowledge that there is still much traditional preaching in the *púlpito*, and why. The factors contributing to this traditional preaching are many.

First of all, many Hispanic preachers have been trained with a pedagogical method that fosters and encourages repetition rather than creativity. Such methods are still prevalent in many of the countries of origin of recent immigrants. They are also prevalent in the *institutos bíblicos* where many Hispanic preachers are formed. Many textbooks for biblical courses tell the students what the Bible says, rather than teaching them how to read it with responsibility and creativity. The same is true of many of the textbooks on theology, whose purpose is to teach the student a list of orthodox doctrines, and the arguments to support them, rather than teaching how to think theologically.

Second, quite often homiletics is taught in the same manner. Even when acknowledging the possibility and value of different approaches to a sermon, most books on homiletics employed in these courses offer set structures, and some even go so far as to provide sermon outlines. (Indeed, books of sermon outlines and illustrations classified by topic sell quite well among Hispanic preachers.)

Third, even in those more advanced schools that pride themselves on the use of more sophisticated methods of biblical study, the hermeneutical task has been neglected. Proponents of the historical-critical method, and of its many later variants, have seemed to imply that such methods will tell us what a text means, apparently forgetting that meaning is always meaning *for the reader*. As a result, even in schools that claim to promote a "critical" reading of the biblical text, this is understood within the very narrow confines of the experiences and perspectives of those who teach. Such a "critical" reading, by its very claim to objectivity, tends to preclude other readings as "acritical" or even "precritical."

Fourth, also in those more sophisticated schools, as well as in many of the churches that served as models for many Latino and Latina preachers, for several decades a sort of preaching was prevalent that did not take the scriptural text seriously. Preaching was mostly about cultural values disguised with a biblical veneer. The implication was that the Bible had little new to say, and that therefore wrestling with a text from the stance of one's own situation would not be very productive.

The result has been that, no matter what their levels of education, many—and probably most—Hispanic preachers are of the traditional sort. Some are fundamentalist, and some are liberal; but neither of the two groups really wrestles with Scripture and with theology in order to hear a new word to deliver to their congregations.

On the other hand—and this is what interests us here—there is a growing number of Latino and Latina preachers who are approaching the *púlpito* with a radically different stance. No matter what their level of education—for one finds them both among seminary graduates and among those who have had almost no formal study—they are taking the situation of their people seriously, and reading the biblical text in a new way.

This is not as alien to Hispanic religiosity, nor as radically new, as it may sound. Although Protestant Latinos and Latinas have been taught to find in the Bible certain things and not others, they have also been taught to approach the Bible, not as a dead document, but as a living word. Even the most conservative Hispanics, when they open the Bible, expect to hear something new. That is why they open and read it regularly. While it is true that this "something new" which they expect is often limited by traditional interpretations that teach them to read Scripture in terms of individual religiosity and morality, it is also true that the expectation that the Bible will speak provides the opportunity for new readings and interpretations.

This is not purely theoretical. Indeed, the reason why the new preaching from the *púlpito* is being generally well received by Latino congregations is precisely that these congregations expect the Bible to speak, and what the preacher is doing—if it is done well—is simply allowing the Bible to speak in a new way to a new situation.

At this point, it is important to point out that to reinterpret a tradition or a text does not mean that one discards them, but on the contrary, that one grants them enough authority and freedom to allow them so speak afresh to a new situation. Elsewhere, I have compared the situation with that of a group of people looking at a landscape.[1] The landscape is there, and cannot be manipulated at whim. Yet the landscape is never seen except from a specific perspective. Every view of the landscape is affected by the position from which it is seen; and yet few would argue that this denies the reality and final authority of the landscape.

Something similar is being discovered and affirmed by a growing number of Hispanic preachers. Most of us have been taught a way of looking at the landscape that is not ours. We have been told what the Bible says, and have also been told, somewhat more subtly, that this is all it says. Thus, we have been unwittingly discouraged from reading and interpreting the Bible and its doctrines on our own. The result has been a rather unauthentic preaching—much as if someone standing in a valley tried to paint the landscape as seen from a mountaintop. This sort of preaching, and the theology behind it, are still quite common in Hispanic pulpits—indeed, they are typical of the first of the two sorts of preacher described above.

The New Shape of Our Theology

The preachers whose work we are attempting to describe are precisely those who have discovered that a different way of looking at the landscape is not only possible, but also necessary for authentic preaching. They approach Scripture with at least as much respect as any other preacher, but also with a measure of suspicion as to what they have been told that Scripture says. Likewise, they approach theology, and every heading of doctrine, with a similar suspicion, asking themselves what particular perspectives a given doctrine or theological position reflects.

One could argue that there are sound theological bases for this attitude, at least under two headings: the doctrine of incarnation and the canon of Scripture.

The central doctrine of the Christian faith is the doctrine of incarnation. A long time ago, commenting on how Neoplatonism had led him to the Christian faith, Augustine said that among the writings of the Neoplatonists he had found the affirmation that in the beginning was the Word, and that the Word was with God, and even that the Word was God. He also found in those writings the claim that through that Word all things were made, and the Word was the light of humankind that illumines everyone who comes to this world. But, Augustine concludes: "What I did not find in them was that this Word was made flesh and dwelt among us."[2] In other words, that the one doctrine that is unique and characteristic of our faith is that God reveals Godself to us by becoming one of us.

This implies that, in order to be truly Christian theology, theology must be incarnate. And this implies that it must take flesh in each culture and situation, in each time and circumstance. Even though certainly the Christian faith is one, it cannot be understood, expressed, and lived out otherwise than in a thousand different ways, according to each time and circumstance. Hence the importance of taking into account the contextual nature of all theology, as well as the need for the Hispanic *púl-pito* to read anew the ancient texts and the traditional theological doc-trines, in order to be truly incarnate.

The second heading that provides a foundation for our own reading of the text is the canon itself of Scripture. The very fact that our New Testament includes four *different* Gospels, yet all attesting to the same truth, shows that the need to take into account the perspective of the observer—and even a variety of perspectives—is central to the very man-ner in which the Bible understands and presents truth.[3] Just as there is a Gospel "according to Matthew" and another "according to Luke," and yet they all witness to the same gospel, so today each of us must preach the gospel from our own perspective, and incarnate it in our own situation.

A Theology That Is Ours

Both of these central points—incarnation and canon—point to the first issue that Latina and Latino preachers face as we seek a theology to inform the *púlpito*: that *theology must be ours* without ceasing to be *uni-versal*. Unfortunately, what passes for universality often is little more than the perspective of the majority, or of those in power, imposed on the rest. This can be seen in a number of contexts. For instance, when men the-ologize, what they produce is called, quite simply, "theology"; but when women theologize, their production is labeled "women's theology." The truth is that men's theology is just as much affected by our gender as is women's theology; yet the one implicitly claims for itself the title of "uni-versal" by the simple expedient of labeling the other after its particular-ity. Therefore, when we say that our theology must be "universal," what we mean is that it must be "catholic": that it must make room for the variety of experiences and perspectives that together constitute the catholicity of the church.

The theology that is taught in our seminaries and courses of study, the theology that is read in most of our textbooks, the theology that we have received from our ancestors in the faith, may be very good in other con-texts. Perhaps it also was good in our context some years ago. But it is not ours. It is a theology that we must know and respect, because we are part of a single body of Christ. But if we simply take it wholesale, without question, it can be alienating and counterproductive for the pastoral praxis we are seeking to implement.

A Theology of Affirmation

Second, this theology that is ours, precisely *because* it is ours, must also be *a theology of affirmation*. If we return to our basic theological texts and interpretations we will see how many of them, rather than affirming our right and our duty to be who we are, deny them. The prevalence of this sort of theology has resulted in a preaching that appears to thrive on showing the hearers their unworthiness, and using this as the basis for calling them to repentance and to God. This may be quite suitable for those who, precisely because they belong to the dominant culture, constantly receive messages, both direct and subliminal, to the effect that their culture is good, and so is their lifestyle. But it is not suitable for those who, in a thousand different ways every day, hear that we are not what we ought to be, that our language is not correct, that our culture is not conducive to democracy, that we have much to learn from the dominant culture, that our people are poor through their own fault, and so on.

The message from a good part of dominant theology is counterproductive for a pastoral praxis in our barrios and among our people. All we have to do is turn on the TV or radio in order to listen to a supposed evangelist proclaim the supposedly good news that we are nothing but unclean worms, which are not worth anything. What we hear over the radio and television is based on an entire theological tradition that seems to think that the best way to exalt God is to degrade the human creature—as if God would be greater the more worthless I am.

While we often associate such attitudes with "fire and brimstone" preachers, it is quite common in the dominant culture and its "mainline" churches among those whose theology and preaching appear more sophisticated. In those churches, we may not hear that we are "unworthy worms," but we will certainly be told that we ought not to think too highly of ourselves. Indeed, in some cases one might suspect that preachers are preaching to themselves, and to the temptation to excessive pride that comes with their position of leadership, and fail to recognize how many in their own congregation may be sinning against God, not by thinking too highly of themselves, but by a low self-esteem that prevents them from responding to God's call to new forms of life and ministry.

But worst of all is that when we visit many of our Hispanic churches we hear sermons in which pastors proclaim the unworthiness of brothers and sisters who live crowded in apartments full of rats and roaches, who have nothing but a shack to protect them from nature, and nothing to protect them from "*la migra.*"[4] And still we claim that it is "good news" to tell them that they are worthless! We also hear sermons about suffering and resignation, and how we are not to resist when others act violently against us, while near us we see a woman whose eyes are still black and blue due to the harsh treatment received from her husband.

And most interestingly, that good man who on TV says that we are not worth much is himself very well dressed and very well fed, and even then tells us that this is so because he serves God! And the sophisticated tall-steeple, male, and mainline preacher is quite offended if people do not show him "proper" respect!

✳ In summary, Hispanics at the *púlpito* are seeking to discover and to express a theology of affirmation. This theology looks at every heading of doctrine from the perspective of the Latino community, asks how it affirms or denies God's love for us, and then reinterprets that heading in the light of those criteria. Likewise, it approaches every biblical text with the same spirit and methodology.

A few examples may clarify how this spirit and methodology apply in concrete instances.

(A) Most of us have been taught that the reason for the Fall was humans wishing to be like God. Yet when we read the Bible from a Hispanic perspective, asking questions of affirmation and self-worth, we soon discover that Genesis, where the serpent tells the first human couple that they will be like God, has already told us that they were like God, who had made them after the divine image and likeness (Gen. 1:26-27). Therefore, perhaps the prime and fundamental temptation is not in wanting to be like God, but in forgetting (and in inviting others to forget) that we already are like God. Perhaps amidst rich and powerful churches it may be necessary to warn people of the sin of excessive pride, which leads them to believe that what they have and what they will have and what they are is because they have somehow earned it. But in our churches and our barrios it is more frequently necessary to remind our people that we are made after the image of God, and those who violate, oppress, or undervalue us, violate, oppress, and undervalue the very image of God.

(B) Hispanic preachers and theologians are also calling us to abandon the quite unbiblical notion that the most important aspect of being human is our intellectual life, and that the only function of the body is to sustain that life. It is on the basis of that notion that we imagine that a person who programs computers, the CEO of an enterprise, or a professor of theology are more worthy and must make more money than whoever picks lettuce or washes laundry. The origin of this view is to be found in the Platonic notion of the superiority of the intellect over the body. Let us not forget that Plato himself declared that philosophy is the occupation of the idle, that is, of those who have time to think, because they do not need to work. Those who do not need to work have others who work for them. In Athens, it was slaves, women, and free but poor laborers. Today, it is those who do the dishes, pick lettuce, and make beds in hotels. Our theology, as theology of affirmation, must affirm the value of the whole human life, physical as well as intellectual and spiritual. It must affirm that it is as important to wash dishes as to lead a corporation; to pick lettuce as to write books; to preach from the pulpit as to take care of a sick relative.

A Theology of Solidarity

Third, this theology that is ours and of affirmation must also be a *theology of solidarity*. For a number of historical, economic, and social reasons Christian theology, like the rest of the church, has become hostage to an individualism that contradicts many of the values both of the Bible and of our traditional cultures. In the midst of a culture in which it was taken for granted that one was a Christian by birth, and in reaction to that error, a theology developed which so underscores an individual's relationship with God that it forgets the communitarian character, not only of faith, but also of the very purposes of God.

That is why we speak of *my* salvation, of knowing Jesus Christ as *my personal* Savior, of what God "has done for *me*." All of that is true and very important. But if we forget *our* salvation, *our* Lord, and what God has done for *us*, we are abandoning a fundamental dimension of the gospel of Jesus Christ. It was not without cause that when his disciples asked Jesus to teach them how to pray he told them: "You will pray thus: Our Father ..." That is why to this day believers, even when they appear to be alone, must pray, "*Our* Father." Whoever prays to this God of ours, is never truly alone; not even alone with God. We are always with God and with our community, participating in it, raising it in prayer to the throne of grace.

This theology of solidarity must manifest itself also in the manner in which we understand the various headings of doctrine. As in the case of a theology of affirmation, some examples may help:

(A) The doctrine of the church should be the focal point of this emphasis on solidarity. However, the most common doctrine of the church circulating among our people, and the one we most commonly learn from the culture around us, although it dresses itself in solidarity, in truth is individualistic. We are told repeatedly that we need the church; but the implication is that the purpose of the church is to strengthen the faith of each believer. The ultimate goal is not the church, the community, but rather the individual, "I." Thus I say that without the church I cannot be a Christian, which certainly is true. But I say it taking for granted that the most important thing is that I *be* a Christian, and that God wishes to create a large number of individual Christians, giving us the church as a place of support and strengthening in the faith.

This is similar to the manner in which the dominant culture understands the purpose of society. Society is not seen as a good in itself, but rather as an instrument for the well-being of individuals. If it were possible for the individual to survive, both physically and mentally, without society, the latter would be dispensable. In the dominant culture we see that even when individualism is attacked, what is ultimately valued is the individual. For example, we are told that excessive individualism is bad because it deprives us of social values, without which it is impossible to produce healthy and strong individuals.

Something similar happens with much of our ecclesiology. We argue that the church is necessary, not because it is an object of God's love and part of the divine plan, but rather because it is the incubator in which individual believers are produced and nourished. Thus, even in that which at first seems to be a critique of the pervasive individualism of our society, we remain trapped in the same individualism.

In the New Testament, however, the church is much more that a conglomerate of faithful individuals who gather in order to support and guide each other. The church is the body of Christ. The church is the manner in which Christ exists in the world. First is the body, then the members. Although the body nourishes its members and gives them life, the body does not live for the members, but vice versa. If this is true, while I must certainly give thanks to God for my salvation, I must above all thank God for our salvation, for the salvation of the church, for the fact that, in this world of sin in which we still partake, we can be part of a new creation, of a new body which is nourished by a new reality; in short, of the body of Christ.

(B) Possibly one of the points in which our theology of solidarity and affirmation has something important to contribute to the rest of the church is precisely this understanding of the value of community, as we see it, for instance, in our vision of the family. In the dominant culture, the family is a closed nucleus, with clearly defined borders, and therefore clearly distinguishable from any other similar group. Therefore, although the notion of family in that culture is not individualistic, in the sense that each person has to fend for himself or herself, it is privatistic in the sense that each family is an individual nucleus, within which each person must look out for the good of their particular family. In Latino culture, however, family is very different. The family is an extensive reality, fluid, with imprecise limits, which includes relatives and connections in all sorts of degrees of consanguinity. It is even possible and almost inevitable to belong to more than one family. Therefore, when in the dominant culture one speaks of the relationship between family and church, the church is seen as an aggregate of families, just as society is an aggregate of individuals. In contrast, in Hispanic culture the church is a family. This is reinforced by the fact that many among our people, used as they are to the extended families of their countries of origin, feel a deep need for the sort and quality of relationships that such a family offers. Perhaps it is our task to rediscover and redefine the meaning of the affirmation that the church is the family of God. But that must remain for another essay.[5]

A Theology of Eschatological Subversion

Fourth, ultimately this theology that is ours, of affirmation and solidarity, must also be *a theology of eschatological subversion*. Eschatology has been practically abandoned by the church of the dominant culture, because to them its sounds like fanaticism and intolerance. It is true that in many of our Hispanics churches the eschatology that is taught and preached supports that stereotype, for it is a dispensationalist eschatology, that often reads the Bible as if it were a puzzle or enigma that can only be solved by those who know the clue.

However, the fact that there is bad eschatology does not imply that all eschatology is necessarily bad. On the contrary, eschatology is absolutely necessary for biblical faith, and therefore the theology that will serve as a basis for Hispanic preaching and pastoral praxis has to be eschatological.[6]

What this means is that it has to be a theology of hope. Unfortunately, in many common stereotypes it is thought that eschatology is a matter of fear, when in truth it is a matter of hope. And not any sort of hope, but a hope that continues in spite of all the negative indications coming from the present society and its order—indications telling us that there is no reason for hope.

⁎ No matter how strange it might seem, the fact is that most of us live life, not from the past, but out of the future we expect. At least, it should be thus among believers in Jesus Christ. We live out of a future we expect, a hope we cherish, a purpose that provides meaning. It is thus that we drive along the street, on the basis on where we are going. The same is true of the entirety of life.

Our theology must include a subversive eschatology, because it has to express and produce among our people a firm hope in a future different from the present, in an order of justice and peace, in a society of equality and solidarity; or, as the prophet would say, of a new order in which they shall learn war no more, but will turn their spears into pruning hooks, each will sit under their own fig tree, and no one—not even the U.S. Citizenship and Immigration Services (USCIS)—will make them afraid.

It is from that future, and only on the basis of that future, that our people will dare live as what we are, as daughters and sons of the Great King, as heirs of the only Lord—or, as Don Quixote would say, as servants of God and instruments of divine justice.

The Text That Interprets Us

The purpose of all of this, however, is not simply to gain a new understanding of a biblical passage, or to gain some interest or insight into a point of doctrine. The reason why we interpret the text of Scripture is that in turn that text interprets us. What is ultimately most important is not what we find in the text, but rather that the text finds us—and even finds us out! All of these new readings of texts and doctrines are important because they speak to a number of issues that are central to the Latino community.

This is a crucial point. The preachers whose work we are seeking to describe here are not reading Scripture anew in order to find new interpretations of the text; they are doing so rather in order to find new truth about themselves, about their congregations, about their communities, and about the world at large. Once again, it is important to insist that for the Latino community of faith the Bible is a living Word, whose power lies in that it engages us with God's truth in ways that we could not do by ourselves. When I open the Bible in order to begin preparing a sermon, I fully expect, not just to discover in the text something I had not seen before, but also to see all those around me and myself under a new light. Biblical interpretation is not ultimately about the text, but about the community in which the interpretation takes place, and which in turn is interpreted by the living text.

The Issue of Culture and Language

One of the central issues for that community is culture and language. Since this has much to do with the actual delivery of the sermon, we shall return to it in chapter 4. However, it is important to see it also as a crucial issue for the *púlpito*—an issue that has much to do with the hermeneutical task that we shall be exploring more fully in chapter 3.

Culture is important for us because it is the primary source of our identity. It is also a complex subject. It is complex, first of all, because cultures have no clear and fixed borders. In the case of Hispanics, while in a sense we all belong to the same culture, in another sense there are within our community a vast number of cultures—which, for the sake of clarity, some call subcultures—reflecting our various countries of origin. The traditional foodstuffs, and especially the seasonings, are different. While the language is the same, the inflections, and even some words, are different. Social customs also vary. And yet, when compared with the dominant Anglo culture of the United States, all these various cultures have much in common, and therefore can properly be seen as a single culture. Furthermore, it is in the United States that these cultures meet and mingle in ways that are unknown in Latin America itself, and thus tend to produce a new culture that is a mixture of all—indeed, there is an emerging Latino culture in the United States that, while drawing from all of the above-mentioned subcultures, is unique and quite distinct from all the subcultures from which it has emerged.

Another element to be taken into account with regard to culture is that Latino culture(s) exists in the United States within the context of another culture—a culture that becomes dominant because it holds the centers of power as well as of communication and education. Therefore,

Latino culture in the United States is evolving into something different from any of the cultures of Latin America, and even different from the sum of all those cultures.

These are issues for the Hispanic *púlpito*, because they are issues for the Hispanic church and community. Is the function of the church to preserve a culture? No matter how we might answer that question theoretically, the fact remains that for many Latinos and Latinas that is certainly part of the function of the church. Excluded as they are from most other centers of decision making, such as politics, economics, and education, the older generation of Hispanics is quite ready to exercise control over their local congregation, and to use that control in order to make certain that the church preserves the traditional culture and language. Needless to say, this adds to the unavoidable generational conflicts, for quite often the younger generation resents being forced to speak and act differently than their peers from the dominant culture.

It would be easy to say that the function of the church is not to preserve and defend culture. In a sense that is true. Yet, there are other considerations that complicate the matter. If, as was stated above, our theology must be one of affirmation, and culture is such an important part of who we are, how can we be affirmed if our culture is not affirmed? This is particularly true of those whose culture and traditions are repeatedly ignored or even demeaned by the dominant culture. Thus, culture is a burning issue for the *púlpito* as well as for the Hispanic church at large.

This in turn tends to privilege culture as a paradigm for reading Scripture, and for preaching from it. The paradigm of *mestizaje*, which Virgilio Elizondo has proposed and which has been quite well received among Hispanics, is a cultural paradigm.[7] It helps us understand the strange, *mestizo* character of our culture(s). It also helps us understand why and how we are marginalized, and how that very marginalization may be a source of creativity. On the basis of this paradigm, a number of elements in the biblical narrative are read differently. Elizondo himself reads the relationship between Galileans and Judeans from the perspective of *mestizaje*, and has abundantly shown that this is a fruitful hermeneutical move.

The theme of culture appears repeatedly in Hispanic preaching. It appears implicitly, in that at every turn we have to decide what language to use, and how—a subject to which we shall return in chapter 4. But it also appears explicitly, as much of our preaching has to do with the challenges of living in an alien culture, and also with the matter of the degree to which we should and should not become part of that culture. Also, it is an explicit theme in much of our hermeneutics, as will be seen in chapter 2.

Social, Economic, and Political Issues

Culture, however, is not the only issue impinging on the *púlpito*. There are also a number of social, economic, and political issues. In general, the social and economic condition of most Hispanics in the United States is one of underprivilege. For a number of years, there has been a constant ratio in negative statistics such as unemployment, poverty levels, underschooling, and the like. No matter what the figures might be for the population at large, the figure for the Latino population is constantly one-and-a-half times as high. For instance, when unemployment stands at 8 percent, Hispanic unemployment is at 12 percent; and when the figure for the general population drops to 6 percent, the figure for Hispanics also drops to 9 per cent. The same is true of figures having to do with population living under the poverty line, with school dropout rates, with single-parent households, and so on. Although in recent times this ratio may have begun to change, there is some doubt as to whether this reflects the real situation, or is just a matter of the census undercounting the least privileged among Hispanics. Also, it is important to remember that statistics regarding poverty levels do not take into account the many dependents that some Hispanics have in their countries of origin, and the millions of dollars that are therefore sent to those countries.

These issues also impinge on the *púlpito*. They impinge on it directly, for preachers must be aware that a large part of their congregation is living under these conditions. They also impinge as a hermeneutical paradigm, parallel to the paradigm of *mestizaje*. Just as Hispanic preachers often read Scripture from the perspective of the encounter of cultures, they also often read Scriptures from the perspective of those acquainted with poverty and all its attending consequences.

It is at this point that the *púlpito* is most influenced by Latin American liberation theology, for which the perspective of the poor provides a preferential paradigm for the reading of Scripture. Much of what Latin American liberation theologians and biblical interpreters find in Scripture is thus brought to bear on the Hispanic *púlpito* in this country. Again, as was indicated at the beginning of this chapter, this is done differently depending on whether the audience is mostly poor Hispanics from the barrio, or relatively affluent representatives of the dominant culture. Yet in both cases the perspective of the poor, and an attempt to read Scripture from that perspective, is characteristic of the Hispanic *púlpito*.

It is not necessary to give examples—particularly since the following chapter will deal more specifically with questions of hermeneutics. However, it is important to note that this is most effectively done when, rather than as the overt subject of the sermon, it is an underlying current that permeates all that is said. This means, among other things, that if one listens carefully the theme of poverty and a Christian response to it appears not only in sermons on Amos or the Epistle of James, but also in sermons on the Lord's Prayer, the Twenty-third Psalm, or the Beatitudes. Precisely because it is an underlying issue, the matter of poverty and all its related evils is always present, even though often under the surface.

Immigration and Exile

An issue that is crucial for the Hispanic *púlpito* is immigration. This requires nuancing, for it is not true that most Hispanics are immigrants. Indeed, census figures show that the vast majority of Hispanics in the United States are citizens of this country by birth. Since Puerto Ricans are U.S. citizens, these figures do include people born in Puerto Rico who now live in the United States. (When census figures give the total of Hispanics in the United States, they do not include residents of Puerto Rico.) However, the fact remains that, even apart from Puerto Rican migration, most Hispanics in the United States were born in this country.

It is important to emphasize this point, because the notion that most Hispanics are immigrants is a stereotype. Certainly, recent immigrants are more noticeable because they do not speak English as well and because they tend to live in communities composed mostly of people of the same or similar origin—for instance, there are barrios in New York City that are mostly Dominican, and others in Los Angeles that are mostly Salvadoran. Because immigrants are more noticeable, people tend to think that they are the majority. Also, for political and other reasons, the mass media tend to center their attention on border crossings and illegal immigration. Thus, the common view is that most Hispanics are fairly recent arrivals, and that the growth in the Latino community is mostly due to recent immigration.

While recent immigration has indeed contributed to the growth of the Hispanic community, the fact is that most of that growth is due to fertility and to the young age of the population. The fertility rate among Hispanics is significantly higher than among the rest of the population. At present, the growth rate (fertility less mortality) among Hispanics is almost 3 percent per year—a figure whose significance becomes obvious by simply pointing out that the growth rate for the general population during the famous "baby boom" was 1.8 percent. While this rate is declining, it is expected to remain above "baby boom" rates at least until 2020. By 2040, when the United States as a whole will have reached zero population growth, the Hispanic rate of growth—apart from immigration—will still be 0.9 percent per year. Therefore, it is wrong to imagine that most Hispanics are immigrants, or that if a way were found to halt all immigration this would stop Hispanic population growth.

Furthermore, not all Hispanics are immigrants or even the descendants of immigrants. The annexation of Texas, and then of a large section of the West and the Southwest, brought into the United States a large number of Spanish-speaking people whose families had lived in those lands for generations. They did not cross the border; rather, the border crossed over them. Before annexation, they were Mexicans by nationality; after annexation, the new settlers who discriminated against them called them "Mexicans." Today, their descendants, often mixed with other Latinos and in many cases with the rest of the population, may be counted in the millions.

For all these reasons, when we speak of "immigration" as an issue for the *púlpito*, we say this at various levels. At the most superficial level, immigration is an issue because many in our congregations—and many standing in our *púlpitos*—are themselves immigrants. They face all the issues that have always faced recent immigrants. They need work, shelter, connections, directions, physical and emotional adjustments, and so forth. They also need to learn English, at least to the extent required to be employable. If they do not have documents declaring them to be "legal" immigrants, they must also face fear of all government agencies, lack of public services—to which, even though sometimes entitled, they do not dare have recourse—exploitation by employers, and so on. In some communities, immigration has become an issue for resident Latinos who fear the possible loss of their already underpaid employment.

At a deeper level, immigration and exile become an issue for Hispanics, because most of us—even to the third and the fourth generations—

have emotional and family contacts beyond the borders of the United States. While we may live here, and be fully committed to the issues that engage the generality of the population, we still have ties elsewhere; and these ties lead us to look at issues differently. Much like the Irish who are concerned about issues in Ireland, or the Jews who follow the politics of Israel, we follow the politics, the literature, and in general all the news from Latin America. This raises issues of identity to which we shall return in a moment—after exploring the deepest level at which immigration is an issue for the *púlpito*.

At the deepest level, immigration is an issue at the *púlpito* because, no matter where we were born, and no matter for how many generations our ancestors may have lived in these lands, we are still made to feel as immigrants by the dominant culture. Until fairly recently, signs were fairly common in the Southwest: "No Mexicans or dogs allowed." For those who posted such signs, being a "Mexican" had little to do with one's place of birth. A Euro-American who had arrived in Texas two weeks earlier could easily post such a sign, thereby excluding "Mexicans" whose ancestors had lived there for generations. For all practical purposes, it was the latter, and not the former, who was the "immigrant"—or rather, the "alien."

While such crass discrimination has been declared illegal, and the vast majority of the population opposes and condemns it, there are other forms of exclusion that tell Hispanics that they are immigrants in this country, no matter for how long they or their ancestors have lived here. The history of the nation is still told from Northeast to Southwest, giving short shrift both to our Indian and to our Spanish ancestors—all of whom were part of the "West" to be "won" for freedom and civilization. In all but a few graduate university programs, knowing French or German is considered not only an asset, but also even a requirement, while knowing Spanish is discounted as irrelevant.

In all these ways—and in many more—the Hispanic population in this country is made to feel as an immigrant population. Quite contrary to fact, they are not seen as one of the main streams contributing to the present culture and civilization—nor are they encouraged to see themselves as such.

It is in this deepest sense that the issue of immigration/exile is crucial for the Hispanic *púlpito*. At this deepest level, it becomes a question of identity—which is probably the most burning issue for the *púlpito*, as well as for the Hispanic community at large. For the past two years, a group of

Hispanic scholars in religion, representing several mainline Protestant churches, have been meeting at Perkins School of Theology for a dialogue funded by the Lilly Endowment. The results of this dialogue, recently published, show the degree to which the question of identity is central, at least to "mainline" Protestant Hispanics.[8] Historians, biblical scholars, theologians, and social scientists all came to the conclusion that throughout their dialogue this had been the theme that had appeared most frequently.

The Issue of Identity

Clearly, the question of identity has some common characteristics for all Latinas and Latinos, plus some added features depending on one's denominational affiliation.

In general, identity becomes a burning issue for all of us because we are all, to one degree ore another, bicultural and bilingual. To a large degree, this is what defines us. While some among us speak very little Spanish, and others speak very little English, still part of our Latino identity has to do with being to some degree bilingual. Some of our children may no longer speak Spanish; but for them it still holds the affective power of a language heard at the cradle. Some may prefer to speak Spanish; but if they are to function in this society they must also be able to communicate in English—no matter how broken.

This bilingual and bicultural character of our community is fostered both by continued immigration and by the modern means of communication. Immigration means that we are constantly meeting more recent arrivals, and that they in turn renew our contact with our ancestral language and culture. The modern means of communication make it possible to listen to the radio, or watch television, in Spanish. Indeed, there are Hispanics who have lived in this country for thirty years, and who still watch the news in Spanish, mostly because they are given a slightly different slant, and because they deal more directly with issues and places that are of interest to them. Likewise, the increasing ease in travel—both in time and in expense—implies that many Latinas and Latinos are able to travel periodically to their place of origin, and thus renew their connection with their ancestral culture and language. In more recent times, the ease of communication through the Internet, and the ready availability of news, commentary, and cultural resources, has made that connection stronger and easier to maintain. As a result, the Latino community in the United States, even after generations of living in this country, remains largely bilingual and bicultural.

For those whose lighter complexion and facial features are more European than Amerindian, the question of identity becomes a matter of decision: Do I wish to be considered Hispanic, or not? In those cases where the answer is yes, there is added incentive to cultivate bilingualism and biculturalism.

For some of those whose features make it clear that they are not part of the dominant culture—some because of markedly Amerindian features, others because of their obvious African ancestry, and still others for various combinations of Amerindian, African, and even Asian traits—bilingualism and biculturalism become means whereby they provide a counterbalance to a culture that in many other ways demeans them.

In short, however, for most Hispanics bilingualism and biculturalism, while providing a sense of identity, also make that identity a more complex matter than for monolingual and monocultural persons. Some of us realize that we think differently in one language than we do in the other, or that we act differently in one cultural context than we do in the other. Hence the burning question of identity: Who am I? Who are we?

Questions of religious identity bring in an added factor. For Protestant Hispanics, the issue is how we can be part of a religion that has been so shaped by the dominant culture, and still remain who we are. Protestantism came to us as a call to abandon much that was not life-giving in our culture and religious tradition; but it also came to us as a call to abandon much in our culture that was part of our identity. In a concluding reflection after the dialogue at Perkins School of Theology described above, one of us took the "empty cross," and its contrast to the crucifix, as a symbol to state these polarities, coming to a conclusion where the question of identity is paramount:

> The result of all this is that the phrase "hanging on an empty cross" has both a positive and a negative meaning. On the positive side, we hang from an empty cross in the sense that we cling to it. In the empty cross we have found liberation, not only from sin and death, but also from much that was sinful and deathful in our own culture and environment. We cling to the empty cross as a symbol of Christ's victory over sin and death, which is also our own.

But there is also a negative side to the empty cross. We hang on an empty cross in the sense that we hang from it, that it is we who have been and are being crucified on it—if not individually, at least in our culture, tradition, and identity. The danger of an empty cross is that it will not remain empty for long. In the crucifix, Jesus hangs in our stead. In the empty cross, there is always the danger that it will be our people, our culture and tradition that will hang in Jesus' stead![9]

This sense of crucifixion is quite strong in many Latino Protestant circles. When we participate in activities, meetings, and decisions of our own denominations, we often feel that we have to suspend—or, in stronger words, to crucify—part of who we are in order to be part of the larger reality. Needless to say, the result is that identity is a burning issue for the Latino pulpit!

Something similar is also true of Roman Catholic Hispanics. In their case, there is no doubt that they cling to the tradition of their ancestors, and in that sense are able to claim their identity much more forcefully and unambiguously than their Protestant sisters and brothers. But here too there are questions of identity raised by the dominant form of Catholicism within which Hispanics must function. An example of this may be seen in an article by Gary Riebe-Estrella, S.V.D., vice president and academic dean of the Catholic Theological Union in Chicago. Riebe-Estrella explains that, for a number of reasons, Latin American Catholicism—and therefore also Hispanic Catholicism in the United States, does not center on the Eucharist, but rather on a number of lay-led sacramental and celebrative acts. After briefly describing a popular celebration of the *Virgen de Guadalupe*, he takes a bold stance:

> I would argue that, in actual fact, the Mass is redundant in this celebration, for it simply ritualizes in a form preferred in Northern Hemisphere Catholicism what Latino Catholicism has already ritualized in song and food. Pastoral ministers in the United States, concerned that there be a Mass on the feast so that the central importance of Christ—the divine become human—is highlighted, have failed to understand that the central beliefs of the Catholic faith can be imaged in quite different ways in different cultural worlds and that the prayer forms that express these beliefs can be equally diverse.... As long as Northern Hemisphere Catholicism makes absolutist claims based on the relativity of its own history, Latino Catholicism will always be undervalued as an historical accident in need of correction. The result will be collision. In most such cases, everyone is a loser.[10]

From these words it is clear that Latino Catholicism is also struggling with the question of its own identity—and often struggling also with dominant views and hierarchies that are not completely sympathetic to its experiences and perspectives.

Quite clearly, the issues discussed here are not a complete listing of all the issues that are relevant to the Hispanic *púlpito*. Latinas and Latinos, like any other worshipers, are concerned about their relationship with God, about sound moral decisions, about their own personal crises and those of their loved ones, about the welfare of the church, and about tragedy, pain, and crisis throughout the world. In these concerns, we are not much different from the rest of humankind.

In any case, since the purpose of this essay is to point out what is distinctive about Hispanic preaching, the issues listed will suffice to show that there are some issues and concern which, while not exclusively Hispanic, certainly do shape our lives, and therefore also our hermeneutics and our preaching. In the next chapter we shall explore how this functions in the actual practice of biblical interpretation.

On the other hand—and that is the real purpose of this book—we are convinced that the issues listed above as those that most concern Latinos and Latinas are in fact human issues, and that therefore our experience, our hermeneutical practice, and our preaching may be of value for the church at large and for its approach to the task of preaching.

Notes

1. Justo L. González, *Santa Biblia: The Bible Through Hispanic Eyes* (Nashville: Abingdon, 1996), pp. 11-21.

2. *Conf.* 7.9.

3. Justo L. González, *Out of Every Tribe and Nation: Christian Theology at the Ethnic Roundtable* (Nashville: Abingdon, 1992), pp. 18-26, discusses this matter more fully, relating it to the very notion of "catholicity," by which the early church characterized its canon of the New Testament. It also shows that something very similar can be said about the Old Testament and about the Bible as a whole. A Spanish version of the same argument appears in *Desde el siglo y hasta el siglo: Esbozos teológicos para el siglo XXI* (Decatur, Ga. and México, D.F.: AETH and Ediciones STPM, 1997). The first of these two books is out of print, but the remaining copies are also being distributed by AETH.

4. The name by which Hispanics used to refer to the Border Patrol and the Immigration and Naturalization Service (INS). The INS title was phased out

and added to the Department of Homeland Security under the name U.S. Citizenship and Immigration Services (USCIS).

5. See "In Quest of a Protestant Hispanic Ecclesiology," in José David Rodríguez and Loida I. Martell-Otero, editors, *Teología en Conjunto: A Collaborative Hispanic Protestant Theology* (Louisville: Westminster/John Knox, 1997), pp. 80-97.

6. On this point, Samuel Pagán's *Su presencia en la ausencia* (Miami: Editorial Caribe, 1993) is a good example of what Hispanic theologians are doing. Pagán offers a reinterpretation of the Exile from a Hispanic perspective, and drawing on the resources of the theology of hope.

7. Virgil Elizondo, *Mestizaje: The Dialectic of Cultural Birth and the Gospel* (San Antonio: Mexican American Cultural Center, 1978); *Galilean Journey: The Mexican American Promise* (Maryknoll, N.Y.: Orbis, 1983); *The Future Is Mestizo: Life Where Cultures Meet* (Bloomington, Ind.: Meyer Stone, 1988). (The fact that sometimes he is called "Virgil," and sometimes "Virgilio," is one more example of how *mestizaje* functions.)

8. David Maldonado, Jr., ed. *Protestantes/Protestants: Hispanic Christianity Within Mainline Traditions* (Nashville: Abingdon, 1999).

9. Justo L. González, "Hanging from an Empty Cross: The Hispanic Mainline Experience" in *Protestantes/Protestants*, pp. 293-303.

10. Gary Riebe-Estrella, S.V.D., "Critic's Corner: Latino Religiosity or Latino Catholicism?" *Theology Today*, 54 (1998), pp. 514-15.

CHAPTER THREE

THE BIBLE AT THE *PÚLPITO*

Pablo A. Jiménez

A s evidenced in the preceding chapter, biblical interpretation is central to Hispanic theology. This is true not only of the academy, which has discovered in Scripture a subversive collection of documents written mostly by and for the poor, but also of Hispanic congregations where the Bible is seen as an authoritative document that leads the believer to a closer and deeper relationship with God.

It should not surprise us, then, that the subject of biblical hermeneutics has been addressed over and over by different Hispanic theologians, including the ones writing this volume. Therefore, I will begin the discussion of the subject summarizing the ideas that have been already advanced on the subject. After such summary, I will present a hermeneutical model that can inform the sermon process. Finally, I will illustrate such methodology, studying the narrative of Jesus' encounter with the Mary and Martha of Bethany (Luke 10:38-42).

A Brief Survey of Hispanic Hermeneutics

It would be utterly impossible to describe exhaustively the work of all the Hispanic theologians who have addressed the topic of biblical hermeneutics. Therefore, I only comment on the works of those whom I judge to be the most influential. I refer those readers interested in a fuller treatment of the subject to the many articles, essays, and books mentioned in the bibliography.

Biblical hermeneutics occupies a prominent space in the thought of the theologians who launched the movement that we now call Hispanic Theology. The birth of this theological endeavor is linked to the work of three distinguished scholars: Virgilio Elizondo, Orlando E. Costas, and Justo L. González.

Virgilio Elizondo is a Mexican American Catholic priest who uses the image of Galilee as a key for the development of a Hispanic theology. During his studies in France, Father Elizondo came to realize that Galilee was a borderland—much like his native Texas. Such realization led him to establish a correlation between the *Mestizo*—who is the result of the miscegenation of Spanish *conquistadores*, Native Americans, and Anglo-Europeans—and the Galilean. Therefore, Jesus' life and ministry become an image for the struggles of the Mexican American people who live in the United States. The Mexican-American experience is understood, then, as a modern Galilean journey.[1]

Orlando E. Costas was an outstanding scholar who honed his theological skills while teaching at the Latin American Biblical Seminary (now University) in San José, Costa Rica. After moving to the United States, he began to adapt and translate into English some of the essays that had made him a renowned missiologist not only in Latin America but also in different parts of the world. Being a contextual theologian, Costas saw how the experience of living permanently in the United States modified and enhanced his theology. Once again, the image of Galilee became central to his theology. In his case, the focus was on the Galilee as a *peripheral* region.[2] He then established a correlation between the Galilean and the Hispanic as people who live in the periphery of centers of power. The Hispanic experience is understood, then, as akin to that of Christ, who was crucified outside the gate of Jerusalem.[3] Costas's untimely death did not allow him to develop in full his theological reflection from and for the Hispanic community.

Justo L. González is a historical theologian by trade who soon became a constructive one. As editor of *Apuntes*[4]—the first theological journal solely dedicated to Hispanic issues in the nation—González fostered the development of the movement. His programmatic essay "Prophets in the King's Court"[5] describes Hispanic theology as an endeavor done from "the margins." His emphasis on a marginal and, therefore, countercultural reading of Scripture, led him to propose a methodology for "reading the Bible in Spanish."[6] Later he furthered his contribution to Hispanic hermeneutics with a comprehensive introduction to and survey of the topic titled *Santa Biblia: The Bible through Hispanic Eyes*.[7] This book explores the different metaphors employed by Hispanic theologians and pastors to summarize, communicate, and advance their hermeneutic approaches.

The works of these founding theologians prompted a new generation of Hispanic scholars to address a wide array of issues. In this second stage, we can identify four theologians who have made important contributions to Hispanic biblical hermeneutics. These scholars are: Fernando F. Segovia, Ada María Isasi-Díaz, C. Gilbert Romero, and Francisco García-Treto.

Fernando F. Segovia is an outstanding Cuban-American Catholic scholar whose many writings have followed, commented on, and promoted the development of Hispanic hermeneutics.[8] Segovia advances a "postcolonial" reading of Scripture.[9] A "postcolonial" reading recognizes that we live in a world shaped by centuries of Anglo-European political and cultural hegemony. Now, as the former colonial powers lose their hegemony over the so-called "third world," the sons and daughters of the colonized have come to live in the former metropolis. This explains the critical presence of ever increasing minority groups in the Unites States and Western Europe. It also explains the ethnic struggles in Eastern Europe and Russia. Segovia employs postcolonial theory to interpret the condition of Hispanics in the United States, stating that we live in "diaspora." He then establishes a correlation between the Hispanic diaspora and the biblical images of exile, diaspora, and "otherness."

Ada María Isasi-Díaz, also a Cuban-American Catholic scholar, is the premier Latina theologian in the nation.[10] Her brand of Hispanic feminism is known as *Mujerista Theology*. Mujeristas recognize that, although the Bible has a subversive and liberating core, such message is enveloped in patriarchal and hierarchical garb. Therefore, Isasi-Díaz uses a "canon within the canon" approach to biblical hermeneutics.[11] She affirms that the Bible must be used to promote the critical consciousness of Hispanic women and to enable moral agency.[12] Isasi-Díaz also uses the images of exile and diaspora to establish a correlation between the ancient world and the contemporary Hispanic experience.[13]

C. Gilbert Romero, a Mexican-American, employs biblical images to describe, understand, and reevaluate popular religiosity. Working mostly within his Catholic tradition, he traces the biblical roots of such practices as Ash Wednesday, the *Quinceañera*, the Home Altar, and the *Penitentes*, among others.[14] The nature and function of revelation is the key to his approach to these popular religious practices. Romero sees Scripture and popular religion as different vehicles for divine revelation.

Romero has also made another important contribution to Hispanic hermeneutics. Romero has explored different biblical images of exile, using them to describe the Hispanic condition. For example, in a short but very provocative article[15] he studies the "Apiru" people—a legendary group that revolted against Egyptian authority around the fifteenth century B. C. E. He then suggests becoming "Apiru" as an agenda for Hispanic theology. "Becoming Apiru" means to recognize your marginal status in society and to understand that marginal groups threaten the powers that be.[16] He has also explored "Apocalyptic Imagination," affirming that it helped the early church to face with hope its situation of marginalization.[17] Hispanic theology can use symbolization and imagination to address and overcome the oppression endured daily by the Latino people.

Francisco García-Treto is a Presbyterian biblical scholar who has made important contributions to the field of biblical interpretation.[18] García-Treto wrote an excellent survey of contemporary Hispanic biblical hermeneutics in his essay "Reading the Hyphens."[19] His comprehensive article begins by stating that an "interpretive community" is at work, forging Hispanic hermeneutics. This interdenominational and intergenerational community takes pride in doing *teología en conjunto* (collegial theology). Then, García-Treto defines key concepts such as "U.S. Hispanic Latino" and "Mainline Protestant." Finally, he explores the contributions of several Hispanic theologians to the field.

This section would be incomplete if we did not mention the many writings of Harold Recinos. Although his main field of research is sociology of religion, Recinos has written extensively about reading the Bible from the perspective of the marginalized. His writings explore the meaning of the Bible for those Latinos and Latinas who live in the inner city *barrios* that continue to grow across the United States.[20] He also explores the meaning of the Bible for Latin American people.[21] One of Recino's most important contributions to the field is the way in which he correlates the biblical image of the city with the Hispanic barrios. He calls us to see the (inner) city as a sacred place and to transform it according to the values of the reign of God.

Once again, I must acknowledge that the previous list is tentative and incomplete. I am not commenting on seminal works by Efraín Agosto,[22] Eduardo Fernández,[23] Jorge González,[24] Daisy Machado,[25] Jean-Pierre Ruíz,[26] and Samuel Pagán.[27] Nor am I commenting on the writings of a brand new generation of Hispanic biblical scholars, led by Leticia Guardiola[28] and Aquiles Ernesto Martínez.[29] In any case, our brief survey suggests that the diverse methodologies share a common core. Let us turn our attention to such points of contact.

A Hispanic Hermeneutical Model

As stated earlier, there is much common ground among the different hermeneutical approaches of Hispanic theologians who have researched the topic. The similarities include the following basic ideas:[30]

* (1) The Bible is a liberating text: Hispanic theologians affirm that the core message of Scripture is, in and of itself, liberating and that "the life and struggles of the Hispanic American community, howsoever defined, have been anticipated in the life and struggles of the people of God in the Bible."[31]

* (2) A "reading of resistance": Hispanic theologians call the Latino community to develop an alternative way of reading the Bible. Such "readings of resistance" are politically charged and, thus, subversive, given that they call into question the present social order in the light of the reign of God.

* (3) The eschatological dimension: Hispanic readings of Scripture are highly eschatological. They see the future of the Latino people with a hope paradoxically born out of the painful experiences of the past. Hispanics are called to play a particular role in God's mission, given that the Latino people open bridges of communication between North and South, and between English-speaking and Spanish-speaking America. Ultimately, Hispanic theology is seen as a radical word of both judgment and hope.

In order to better understand the different theological insights surveyed above, I propose a model for interpreting Scripture from a Hispanic perspective. I propose this model with the double aim of systematizing the theological principles analyzed above and of providing a methodology that may inform the sermon preparation process:[32]

(1) Marginalization is the entry point: The first step is pondering the social situation of the Latino people in the United States. The experiences of marginalization, oppression, and discrimination endured by the Latino people serve as the point of entry to the liberating power of the Bible. The particular social location of the Latino people makes possible a liberating dialogue with Scripture. When a Hispanic person reads the Bible, he or she finds a message written by and for the marginalized and the oppressed. This grants Latinos and Latinas a unique access to the "core" of the biblical message.

(2) Seeking points of contact: With the above-mentioned social analysis at hand, we then read to seek in the Bible different points of contact between the social location of the Hispanic community and the biblical narrative.

(3) A correlation of social locations: After finding such points of contact, the model calls us to compare the social location of the Latino community and the social location of the Bible. Such correlation must go beyond a mere "correspondence of terms," exploring a "correspondence of relationships." Let me explain briefly the difference between these approaches. An interpreter looks for the correspondence of terms when he or she correlates biblical concepts with contemporary ones on the basis of language. For example, I recently read a brief commentary on the dedication of Solomon's temple. After sound historical analysis, the author ended by calling the readers to see their church buildings as places of encounter with God. In this case, the author correlated "temple" with "church building," applying the ancient teachings to the modern edifices. This is the kind of reasoning that prompts preachers to say phrases like: "We are just like the children of Israel in the wilderness" and "Aren't we just like the Peter, John, and the rest of the disciples?" To seek correspondences of relationships requires further biblical research, using sociological and anthropological analysis. An interpreter looks for the correspondence of relationships when he or she correlates biblical concepts with contemporary ones on the basis of their functions in society. The key question is: Which contemporary situation works in a way similar to the situation we see in this

biblical text? Let us go back to the example of the temple. Besides being a house of worship, the temple of Solomon was a centralized shrine that organized and regulated the faith of Israel. In this sense, it was the embodiment of the normative or official religion. The temple also had political and economic functions, symbolizing the independence of Israel from other nations (who had their own divinities) and collecting money and goods for the national treasury. In this sense, to compare the building of a local congregation with the Solomonic temple is a mistake. Depending on the function under study, the temple may be compared to the general headquarters of a mainline denomination, to a patriotic monument, or to a national bank. In summary, the correlation of social locations looks for the correspondence between the social relations that underlie and therefore shape the biblical text and the social relations that underlie and shape our experience.[33] This biblical reading does not yield formulas to be copied or techniques to be applied.[34] It offers orientations, models, types, directives, and inspiration. The aim of such reading is to give us elements to be used as tools in the interpretation of both our current reality and the possibilities that the future will bring.[35]

(4) A key metaphor: Hispanic theology employs different metaphors to communicate the implications of the correlation between the social location of the text and the social location of the Latino community. Such metaphor embodies its findings, functioning as a paradigm. In a way, the metaphor summarizes the whole hermeneutical process. Then, the metaphor-turned-paradigm is used to exegete both the Bible and Hispanic reality. The two key metaphors employed by Latino and Latina theologians are "marginality" and *mestizaje*. These metaphors evoke the "correspondence of relations" between the social location of the Bible and the social location of the Latino people discussed above. They can function as paradigmatic concepts because they symbolize and summarize such correlation. In a way—borrowing the jargon of structuralism—it is possible to affirm that each metaphor functions as a "signifier"—the sensible or material component of the linguistic sign—that refers to a "signified," the conceptual component of the linguistic sign.[36] In this case, marginality and

mestizaje are the "signifiers" and the correlation of social locations is the "significant." However, these are not the only "signifiers" that may be used to denote the correspondence in relationships. In his book *Santa Biblia: The Bible Through Hispanic Eyes*,[37] Justo L. González acknowledges the diversity of paradigms employed by Hispanic theologians and Latino pastors in their writings and sermons. After much research, he identifies five metaphors that are used as paradigmatic concepts in Latino theological thought. These are: marginality, poverty, *mestizaje*, exile and alienness, and solidarity.

It is clear that the true key to this hermeneutical model is the correlation between the social location of the Bible and the social location of the Latino people. However, this model can be very useful for non-Hispanic preachers who want to engage the Bible in a new way. In particular, this model fosters a contextual, liberating, and postmodern reading of Scripture.

Mary and Martha of Bethany: A Hispanic Reading of Luke 10:38-42

After studying the basic aspects of Hispanic hermeneutic theory, let us see an example of how to apply such theory.

The Gospels tell us precious little about Jesus' private life. Given that their focus is Jesus' words and ministry, they hardly mention his friends and they do not expound on his family life. Yes, we do know that Jesus called a number of men to be his students or "disciples" (see Luke 6:12-16 and its parallels). And, yes, we do know that a number of women followed Jesus, traveling with the Twelve (Luke 8:1-3). The female disciples were "Mary, called Magdalene, from whom seven demons had gone out, and Joanna, the wife of Herod's steward Chuza, and Susanna, and many others, who provided for them out of their resources" (Luke 8:2b-3). Therefore, although we know who were Jesus' male and female disciples, we know very little about his friends.

We might say that Jesus befriended the family formed by Martha, Mary, and Lazarus from Bethany. The Gospels of Luke and John mention these characters in different places (Luke 10:38-42; John 11:1–12:11, 17). Luke mentions only the sisters. John does mention Lazarus, relating his death, his resurrection, the celebration of the Passover at this house, and the plot to kill him. In that scenario, Mary and Martha are supporting characters who mourn their brother's death and who rejoice in his resurrection. Nonetheless, we find important points of contact between the Lukan and the Johannine portrayal of the sisters. Both Luke 10:38-42 and John 12:1-7 describe meals at the family house. The Lukan meal is a private affair; the Johannine one is a community banquet. In both stories Martha is in charge of serving the meals, a service described by the Greek word *diakonia* in Luke 10:40 (translated in the NRSV as "tasks" and "work") and in John. 12:2 (translated in the NRSV as "served"). In both stories Mary is at Jesus' feet, listening to his teachings in Luke 10:39 and anointing him in John 12:3. In both stories Mary's attitude is criticized, by Martha in Luke 10:40 and by Judas Iscariot in John 12:4-6. In both stories Jesus justifies Mary's behavior (Luke 10:41-42 and John 12:7).

Here is the Lukan account of Jesus' visit to Mary and Martha of Bethany:

> Now as they went on their way, he entered a certain village, where a woman named Martha welcomed him into her home. She had a sister named Mary, who sat at the Lord's feet and listened to what he was saying. But Martha was distracted by her many tasks; so she came to him and asked, "Lord, do you not care that my sister has left me to do all the work by myself? Tell her then to help me." But the Lord answered her, "Martha, Martha, you are worried and distracted by many things; there is need of only one thing. Mary has chosen the better part, which will not be taken away from her." (Luke 10:38-42)

This biblical story is very well known, appearing regularly in different lectionaries.[38] The details of the story are rather straightforward:

(1) Jesus arrives at the village.

(2) Martha offers him hospitality.

(3) Mary sits at Jesus' feet to hear his teachings.

(4) Martha asks Jesus to instruct Mary to help her in the preparation of the meal and the service at the table *(diakonia)*.

(5) Jesus answers Martha, stating that she is worried and burdened "by the many" (Gk. *peri polla*). Meanwhile, only "the one"

(Gk. *enos*) is needed. This reading is, certainly, enigmatic. As usually happens with such readings, several ancient manuscripts offer alternative wording that may clarify, soften, or even change the meaning of the text. In this case, some readings use the Greek verb *turbazomai* instead of the rare *thorubazo*, given that both mean to be worried, confused, or afflicted. Other readings change the word "the one" for "a few" (Gk. *oligon*). Still other readings omit the last part of the phrase.

(6) Jesus justifies Mary's choice, affirming that she chose the "good" or "better part, which will not be taken away from her" (v. 42*b*).

The traditional interpretation of this biblical text sees Martha and Mary as symbols of different approaches to the Christian life. One represents action and the other introspection. Thus, sermons that follow this interpretive line uphold Mary of Bethany as the embodiment of the contemplative life. Such sermons conclude calling us to be like the devoted Mary, not like the busy Martha.

Sadly, we must acknowledge that some sermons on this text preach against the text, criticizing Mary's choice. These sermons expound on the importance of action and of "taking care of business." The preachers who craft such sermons are usually males who are betrayed by their hidden patriarchal ideas. Therefore, they uphold "Martha" as the archetypal housewife (although the text portrays her as a single woman) who, by definition, is the ideal caretaker.

Recently, these traditional approaches to the text have been challenged in different ways. For example, several female biblical scholars call our attention to the use of the word *diakonia* in the text. They correctly state that this word—that originally meant the service at the table—became one of the key technical terms employed by the New Testament to denote the Christian ministry. This Greek expression is the root of English words like "deacon" and "deaconess." This fact raises the disturbing possibility that the criticism of Martha's *diakonia* may be a general criticism of women's leadership in the Christian community.[39]

Elisabeth Schüssler Fiorenza's detailed analysis of this text follows a similar interpretive line.[40] She criticizes the "abstractionist" interpretations that reduce Mary and Martha to symbols of theological principles. She also criticizes the "apologetic" and the "psychological" interpretations that try to save the text by affirming or focusing, respectively, on women's access to theological education and sibling rivalry. At the end, Schüssler Fiorenza concludes that Luke intended to undercut women's discipleship.[41] She calls us to engage in a hermeneutics of evaluation and proclamation that acknowledges the patriarchal penchant of the text, affirms its subversive elements (i.e., Mary's audacity), and reenvisions women's ministries as practices of solidarity and justice.

After this brief survey of possible interpretations of the text, let us re-engage the text from a Hispanic perspective using the hermeneutic model described above.

Marginalization Is the Entry Point

As stated earlier, Hispanics are a largely marginalized community in the United States. Even the government, through institutions such as the Bureau of the Census, acknowledges the poverty and oppression lived daily by Latinos and Latinas in the nation. For example, according to the estimates of the Census for 2000, only 57 percent of Hispanics have a high school diploma; only 11.1 percent have a college degree; 8.1 percent are unemployed, 21.4 percent live under the poverty line; and 28 percent of Hispanic children live in poverty. These numbers compare unfavorably to the 88.7 percent of white Euro-Americans who have completed their high school education; the 27 percent who have a college degree; their 5.1 per cent unemployment rate; and the 7.8 percent who live under the poverty line.

The poverty and marginalization of the Hispanic community forces the Latino people to work very hard for little money in the agricultural and service industries. The poorest of the poor Hispanics work as migrant agricultural workers, gardeners, custodians, and nannies. Many, prompting the development of stereotypes that further oppress and marginalize the Latino community, see these honorable endeavors with contempt. They have somehow concluded that our place is the kitchen, the garden, or the nursery.

This sad fact of life directs Hispanics to read the story of Jesus' visit to Mary and Martha with different eyes. We can relate to the marginalized women of biblical times because we are marginalized today. In Jesus' time, most Jewish women were poor. They lived under a patriarchal system that largely relegated them to the kitchen and to the household. Even their religion relegated them to secondary roles, given that they could not be circumcised and they did not have access to the priesthood. Yet, recent scholarship has established with certainty that, under some circumstances, some women had access to social and religious leadership.[42] Such research reminds us that some Jewish sects welcomed women, treating them as equals.[43] Apparently the Essenes were open to women's discipleship, allowing them to participate in ritual washings and encouraging their participation in the communal study of Scripture. There is also archaeological evidence of Jewish women leading synagogues as early as the third century. Nonetheless, the fact remains that most women were excluded from social and religious leadership.

Therefore, a Hispanic reading of this text would correlate the marginality of the sisters in the Jewish world with the marginal status of the Latinos in the United States.

A *"Reading of Resistance"*

The second step in our model is to develop a "reading of resistance" that would affirm the liberating aspects of the text. This step calls us to find points of contact between the biblical story and the Latino experience.

When we read this biblical story as an account written for and from marginalized people, the story of Mary and Martha is truly subversive. In a world dominated by men, Martha and Mary are portrayed as single women. The Lukan account—which does not mention Lazarus—is very suggestive. Could Martha have been a widow who had inherited her family dwelling? If this were the case, Martha would be the older sister. In contrast, Mary would be the younger single sister. We must remember that Jewish women married very young, around 14 years old at the latest. Could we infer, then, that Mary was under that age?

In any case, Mary relates to Jesus as a disciple would, sitting at his feet to hear his teachings (compare with Acts 22:3). Her stance demonstrates audacity at many levels. First, it defies women's exclusion from rabbinical discipleship. This exclusion is well documented in later Judaism.[44] As stated before, such exclusion was not universal in Jesus' times. However, most religious leaders practiced it. Therefore, in sitting at Jesus' feet, Mary defies religious conventions that ban women from rabbinical training.

Mary also defied social conventions, particularly the practices that regulated modesty. We know that ancient Jewish society, as do contemporary Islamic ones, discouraged public exchanges between males and females. In this case, we have two (unmarried?) women offering hospitality to an unmarried man. Further, we must remember that in the average Palestinian house food was cooked outside, in an earthen oven.

Therefore, Mary appears to be alone with Jesus while Martha is cooking outside. At this point, we must also remember that to sit at someone's feet was the proper attitude of a male disciple. There is a well-known biblical story where a woman lies at a man's feet in order to seduce him:

> Now wash and anoint yourself, and put on your best clothes and go down to the threshing floor; but do not make yourself known to the man until he has finished eating and drinking.... Then she came stealthily and uncovered his feet, and lay down. At midnight the man was startled, and turned over, and there, lying at his feet, was a woman! (Ruth 3:3, 7b-8)

This is, of course, the story of Ruth, who seduces Boaz under Naomi's advice.

It should not surprise us then that Martha finds Mary's actions inappropriate. After all, she is crossing several social boundaries. We must notice that Martha words her petition very carefully because she does not want to dishonor Jesus. Instead of calling into question the implications of her sister's stance, she defers to Jesus, granting him decision power over the family. He, as the patriarchal male figure, must tell Mary to go help in the kitchen. It is a subtle way of asking Jesus to put Mary in her place without questioning his judgment or his intentions.

Hispanics can relate to the story at many levels. We face daily social boundaries drawn in order "to keep us in our place." We are underrepresented in institutions of theological education, most of which do very little to reach Latinos and Latinas. We are considered emotional, passionate, and even violent people. The stereotypical image of the Latin lover or the Latina sexpot is furthered by the portrayal of Hispanics in the media. While the larger society benefits from our work, many want us to remain segregated and, therefore, invisible.

The text not only appeals to Hispanics for its treatment of social boundaries. Honor is another topic important to the Latino people. As Ismael García clearly explains in his book *Dignidad*,[45] personal honor and dignity are pivotal concepts in Hispanic American culture. Even though she complains, Martha offers Jesus a subtle way out of an embarrassing situation, allowing both Mary and him to "save face."

A Correlation of Social Locations

In this study, I have tried to establish a correlation between the social location of the characters portrayed in the text and the social location of the Hispanic community. Notice that such correlation takes into consideration social and economic forces, not a mere correspondence of wording. This correlation allows us to transcend even the gender boundaries that taint the analysis of this biblical passage. Latinos and Latinas can relate to the situation of marginalization faced by Mary and Martha. Most male and female Hispanics have been asked at some time to go back to the "kitchen" and to "stay in their place." All Hispanics face social boundaries and most are criticized when they try to transcend them.

One of the most insidious problems faced by Hispanic people is the internalization of the social boundaries that have been pressed upon us along the years. As demonstrated by Albert Memmi,[46] oppressive situations foster ideas of helplessness in the oppressed. Memmi describes the mentality of the "colonized" who end up believing that they are inferior to the "colonizer." Through an oppressive socialization process, the marginalized accepts unjust social boundaries as "normal." In this text, Martha voices a view that upholds the traditional roles of women. In affirming Mary, Jesus is equally affirming Martha's right to transcend the social boundaries that kept her "in the kitchen."

Hispanics must also transcend the "colonized" mentality that has been and is internalized through different socialization processes. Yes, we are largely invisible in grade school curricula. However, the problem is compounded by stereotypical portrayals in the media that depict us as drug addicts, drug dealers, criminals, prostitutes, or unemployed welfare dependents. A number of Hispanics, deceived by these socialization processes, end up believing that they are indeed morally corrupt and intellectually inferior.

Marginality: A Key Metaphor

We can, therefore, use the term "marginality" as a key metaphor to understand, exegete, and interpret this text. Jesus relates to marginalized persons (poor women in a patriarchal society). He affirms the marginalized as they break rules and cross social boundaries. He announces that God wants to relate to the poor. He calls the marginalized to develop and enjoy a relationship with God.

In conclusion, let us focus on the phrase "there is need of only one thing" (v. 42a). When we think about the use of the number one in Scripture, our minds wander to Deuteronomy 6:4: "Hear, O Israel: The LORD our God is one LORD" (RSV). This phrase marks the beginning of a key biblical section (vv. 4-9) known as the *Shema* (the first word of the phrase is the verb meaning "to hear and obey"). Parts of this confessional affirmation were taken literally, giving rise to the use of phylacteries, small leather boxes containing little scrolls with Exodus 13:1-16 and Deuteronomy 6:4-9; 11:13-21 written on them. They were placed "as a sign on your hand, fix them as an emblem on your forehead, and write them on the doorposts of your house and on your gates" (Deut. 6:8-9). Thus, most Jewish people knew these biblical verses by heart.

I propose, then, that we should read Jesus' response to Martha in the light of the *Shema*. If this is so, then Luke 10:42 is calling the Christian community to "keep these words that I am commanding you today in your heart" (Deut. 6:6). This call to hear and heed God's word would be consistent with Luke 8:15 and 21. Finally, we must notice that Luke refers directly to the *Shema* in the Parable of the Good Samaritan, the story that immediately precedes the one on Mary and Martha. Luke 10:27 quotes Deuteronomy 6:5, joining it with Leviticus 19:18.

In this sense, we should read jointly the Parable of the Good Samaritan and the story of Jesus' encounter with Mary and Martha. Both stories use marginalized characters whose faith compels them across social borders. The former answers the question: "Who is my neighbor?" The latter answers the question: "Who can be a disciple?" Jesus' response is that a disciple is a person who "keeps God's words" (see Deut. 6:6; Luke 8:15, 21). Ethnicity, gender, or any other social barrier does not define participation in the Christian community. The true disciple is the person who is radically committed to "the One God."

Notes

1. Elizondo, *Galilean Journey.*

2. See Orlando E. Costas, "Evangelism from the Periphery: The Universality of Galilee" in *Voces*, pp. 16-23 and *Liberating News.*

3. Orlando E. Costas, *Christ Outside the Gate* (Maryknoll: Orbis, 1989).

4. *Apuntes: Reflection from the Hispanic Margin* is published by the Perkins School of Theology's Mexican American Program at Southern Methodist University, Dallas, Texas.

5. *Apuntes* 1:1 (Spring 1981): 3-6. It is also the opening essay of *Voces.*

6. González, *Mañana*, pp. 75-87.

7. Nashville: Abingdon, 1996.

8. Fernando F. Segovia, "Hispanic American Theology and the Bible: Effective Weapon and Faithful Ally" in *We Are a People*, pp. 21-49; "Reading the Bible as Hispanic Americans" in Leander Keck, editor, *The New Interpreter's Bible*, Vol. 1 (Nashville: Abingdon Press, 1994); "Two Places and No Place on Which to Stand: Mixture and Otherness in Hispanic American Theology" in Arturo Bañuelas, editor, *Mestizo Christianity: Theology from the Latino Perspective* (Maryknoll: Orbis, 1995), pp. 28-43; "Toward a Hermeneutics of the Diaspora: A Hermeneutics of Otherness and Engagement" in Fernando F. Segovia and Mary Ann Talbert, editors, *Reading from This Place, Vol. 1: Social Location and Biblical Interpretation* (Minneapolis: Fortress, 1995), pp. 57-73.

9. Fernando F. Segovia, *Decolonizing Biblical Studies: A View from the Margins* (Maryknoll: Orbis, 2000).

10. For a comprehensive introduction to her thought see *En la Lucha/In the Struggle: Elaborating a Mujerista Theology* (Minneapolis: Fortress, 1993).

11. Here I follow Segovia's analysis in *We Are a People*, pp. 30-33.

12. See "The Bible and *Mujerista* Theology" in Susan Brooks Thistlewaite and Mary Potter Engel, editors, *Lift Every Voice: Constructing Christian Theologies from the Underside* (San Francisco: Harper Collins, 1990).

13. See her exegetical essay "By the Rivers of Babylon: Exile as a Way of Life" in *Reading from This Place, Vol. 1*, pp. 149-63 and in Isasi-Díaz's *Mujerista Theology* (Maryknoll: Orbis, 1996), pp. 35-56.

14. C. Gilbert Romero, *Hispanic Devotional Piety: Tracing the Biblical Roots* (Maryknoll: Orbis, 1991).

15. C. Gilbert Romero, "On Becoming 'Apiru': An Agenda for Hispanic Theology," *Apuntes* 16:2 (Summer 1996):59-61.

16. Ibid., p. 61.

17. C. Gilbert Romero, "Hispanic Theology and Apocalyptic Imagination," *Apuntes* 15:4 (Winter 1995):133-37.

18. See, for example, "The Lesson of the Gibeonites: A Proposal for Dialogic Attention as a Strategy for Reading the Bible" in *Hispanic/Latino Theology*, pp. 73-85. See also "The Book of Nahum: Introduction, Commentary, and Reflections" in *The New Interpreter's Bible*, Vol. VII, pp. 591-619.

19. Francisco García-Treto, "Reading the Hyphens: An Emerging Biblical Hermeneutic for Hispanic U.S. Protestants" in David Maldonado, Jr., editor, *Protestantes/Protestants: Hispanic Christianity Within Mainline Traditions* (Nashville: Abingdon, 1999), pp. 160-71.

20. For a brief introduction to Recinos's "Barrio Theology" see "Mission: A Latino Pastoral Theology," *Apuntes* 12:3 (Fall 1992):115-26. For a more comprehensive approach, see *Jesus Weeps: Global Encounters on Our Doorsteps* (Nashville: Abingdon, 1992).

21. *Who Comes in the Name of the Lord? Jesus at the Margins* (Nashville: Abingdon, 1997).

22. "Social Analysis of the New Testament and Hispanic Theology: A Case Study," *Journal for Hispanic/Latino Theology* 5:4 (1998):6-29. See also the essay "Paul, Leadership and the Hispanic Church" in Eldin Villafañe, editor, *Seek the Peace of the City* (Grand Rapids: Eerdmans, 1995).

23. "Reading the Bible in Spanish: U.S. Catholic Hispanic Theologians' Contribution to Systematic Theology," *Apuntes* 14:3 (Fall 1994):86-91.

24. *Daniel: A Tract for Troubled Times* (New York: General Board of Global Ministries, 1985).

25. "El Cántico de María," *Journal for Preachers* 21:1 (1997):12-15.

26. "Beginning to Read the Bible in Spanish: An Initial Assessment," *Journal for Hispanic/Latino Theology* 1:2 (1994):28-50.

27. "The Book of Obadiah: Introduction, Commentary, and Reflections" in *The New Interpreter's Bible*, Vol. VII, pp. 433-59.

28. "Borderless Women and Borderless Texts: A Cultural Reading of Matthew 15:21-28," *Semeia* 78 (1997): 69-81.

29. "El Apóstol Pablo y la comunidad de Tesalónica," *Apuntes* 15:1 (Spring 1995):3-13.

30. In this section I follow Fernando F. Segovia, "Hispanic American Theology and the Bible: Effective Weapon and Faithful Ally" in *We Are a People*, pp. 45-49.

31. Ibid., p. 46.

32. I have addressed these issues before in José D. Rodríguez and Loida I. Martell-Otero, editors, "The Bible: A Hispanic Perspective" in *Teología de Conjunto: A Collaborative Protestant Theology* (Louisville: Westminster/John Knox Press, 1997), pp. 66-79; and "In Search of a Hispanic Model of Biblical Interpretation," *Journal of Latino/Hispanic Theology* 3:2 (November 1995):44-64.

33. Clodovis Boff, *Teología de lo político: Sus mediaciones* (Salamanca, Spain: Ediciones Sígueme, 1980), p. 278.

34. Ibid., p. 279.

35. Ibid., p. 280.

36. Stephen D. Moore, *Poststructuralism and the New Testament: Derrida and Foucault at the Foot of the Cross* (Minneapolis: Fortress, 1994), p. 132. For further information on these concepts see Roland Barthes, *Elements of Semiology* (New York: The Noonday Press, 1973), pp. 35-57, passim.

37. Nashville: Abingdon, 1995.

38. For example, Luke 10:38-42 is the Gospel reading for the eleventh week after Pentecost (Proper 11) in the Year C of the Revised Common Lectionary. It is also the reading for the Friday on the seventh week of Easter; the third Sunday after Pentecost; and the Friday of the twenty-fourth week after Pentecost in the Anglican Daily Office Lectionary, among others.

39. Jane Schaberg, "Luke" in *The Women's Bible Commentary*, edited by Carol A. Newsom and Sharon H. Ringe (Louisville: Westminster/John Knox, 1992),

pp. 288-89. See also Barbara E. Reid, *Choosing the Better Part? Women in the Gospel of Luke* (Collegeville, Minn.: The Liturgical Press, 1996), pp. 144-62.

40. *But She Said: Feminist Practices of Biblical Interpretation* (Boston: Beacon, 1992), pp. 52-76.

41. Ibid., p. 64.

42. See, for example, Sarah B. Pomeroy, *Goddesses, Whores, Wives, and Slaves: Women in Classical Antiquity* (N.Y.: Schocken Books, 1975).

43. For an introduction to the topic, see Amy L. Wordelman, "Everyday Life: Women in the Period of the New Testament" in *The Women's Bible Commentary*, pp. 390-96.

44. See the rabbinical references in Albercht Oepke, *"gunē,"* in Gerhard Kittel, editor, *Theological Dictionary of the New Testament*, Vol. I (Grand Rapids: Eerdmans, 1964), pp. 781-82.

45. *Dignidad: Ethics Through Hispanic Eyes* (Nashville: Abingdon, 1997).

46. *The Colonizer and the Colonized*, expanded edition (Boston: Beacon, 1991).

CHAPTER FOUR

Standing at the *Púlpito*

Justo L. González

Preaching as a Communal Event

Having explored the process by which a text is brought to bear on
the *púlpito*, we now come to the actual point at which the sermon is
delivered. This is crucial, for most Hispanics do not see the sermon as
a text, but rather as an event. Just as music written on a pentagram is
not music until it is played, so words written in a manuscript do not
become a sermon until they are preached. Although usually the manuscript is chronologically prior to the act of preaching, what makes a
text *be* a sermon is not that it is written, but rather that it is preached.
Once again, the comparison with music may be helpful. Although it
is quite normal for a composer to write the score for a composition
before it is performed, other composers play the piece first and then
have it written. In neither case is the written score the same as the
musical piece. The score may be an important way to communicate
the content of the piece to others who may not be able to hear it, or
to remind those who have heard it; but a score that is never played is
not real music. Likewise, a preacher may or may not write a sermon
before she preaches it; but in no case is the written text the same as
the act of preaching—and it is only that act that can turn the words
written in a manuscript into an actual sermon.

Furthermore, this act is communal. Although quite clearly in most situations the preacher speaks and the congregation listens, this does not mean that the preacher is active and the congregation passive. On the contrary, the best Hispanic preachers are those who, even at the very moment of preaching, can "hear" the congregation's audible and inaudible responses. And a congregation that really listens finds ways to communicate to the preacher what it is hearing. In Hispanic churches, this is often done in ways similar to the traditional practice in African American churches: by means of verbal responses such as "Amen" or "Alleluia." It is also done by means of gestures such as raising of hands, waving bulletins or handkerchiefs, and by more emotional expressions such as tears, sighs, and laughter—or by vacant eyes and heads nodding in sleep!

By all of these means, the congregation is communicating to the preacher that it recognizes—or does not recognize—the Word of God in the preacher's words.

The preacher in turn must be able to hear what the congregation is saying, and respond to it. This is one reason why Hispanic preachers are so often surprised by the frequent confusion in the dominant culture between a manuscript for a sermon and an actual sermon. Most Hispanic seminarians are puzzled when they receive the assignment to "write" a sermon—not because they think that a sermon should not be well thought out, or because they object to the attempt to write what one intends to say, but rather because if one believes that the written piece is the sermon, one will not be able to enter into a true give and take with the congregation, and the sermon, rather than an act, will become a literary piece. Changing our imagery from the musical to the culinary, one could say that a written text is to a sermon as a recipe is to a dish: it provides guidance for the actual cooking, but the recipe in and of itself, without the proper ingredients, fire, and timing, would be rather insipid!

To say that the sermon is a communal event is also to amplify Arrastía's notion of the congregation as a hermeneutical community to the congregation as a homiletic community.[1] Just as good preachers do their hermeneutical task in conversation with the congregation and its experiences and perspectives, so do they perform their homiletic task in a similar conversation.

As a result, in the *púlpito* there is a clear difference between elegance and eloquence. Elegance is a beautiful turn of phrase, creative imagery, proper use of language. These are indeed valuable, and are improved by the written text. But eloquence is the ability to communicate with a congregation—a communication that must necessarily flow in both directions.

The Practice of Preaching from the *Púlpito*

To say that the sermon is a communal act means that issues of setting and delivery are not peripheral to the sermon. They are not mere "techniques" that one learns to apply to the "sermon" one has already written. On the contrary, they are an integral part of the sermon. The preacher must take the setting into account, not only in preparing the sermon, but also in the very act of preaching. Items such as the use of language, voice, and gesture are not mere adornments, but a constitutive element of the sermon.

For these reasons it will be important for our readers to know something about the normal setting and practice of Hispanic preaching.

One item that surprises many Euro-American pastors in the "mainline" denominations is the frequency of preaching in the Latino church. It is not unusual for a pastor to preach three or four times a week to the same congregation—plus lead at least one Bible study, one Sunday school class, and probably offer some other "evangelistic" preaching outside the church building. Hispanic Protestants have taken the Reformation's emphasis on the preaching of the word to the point that there can hardly be a service—sometimes even those advertised as "prayer services"—without preaching—or at least a brief homily.

Hispanic preaching is not only frequent; it is also lengthy. Although at present there is a tendency in some circles to reduce the length of a sermon, forty minutes is not usually considered excessive, and most congregations consider anything less than half an hour too short. (Hispanic preachers who for some reason have become accustomed to the "standard" twenty-minute sermon may have the experience I had recently, after finishing a sermon that was no more than "normal" length by Anglo standards. The pastor stood up and said: "Brother, that is not enough. Feed us more!" The congregation responded with a loud "Amen." I simply had to stand up and preach another twenty minutes.)

The length of the sermon in Latino churches affects both its structure and its preparation. In its structure, a typical Latino sermon varies according to the congregation. If the audience is composed mostly of persons of the dominant culture, and the sermon is expected to last no more than twenty or twenty-five minutes, the structures employed are very similar to those studied in the standard manuals of homiletics. If, on the other hand, the sermon is expected to last at least forty minutes, two things are likely to happen: First, there may be more digressions. It is not unusual for a Hispanic preacher to take a ten-minute detour into a related subject, and then come back to the point. Second, the sermon may attempt to make more than one point—thus losing coherence and perhaps impact. Thus, it is not unusual for a preacher to draw three largely unrelated themes from a single biblical text, and to develop all three in the same sermon.

Still on the matter of structure, a good Hispanic preacher knows that the congregation will find it hard to listen for forty minutes to an hour, and therefore employs a number of devices that are less common in Anglo sermons. This is one reason why Hispanic preachers tend to be more dramatic, and to appeal to the emotions more than other preachers. Structurally, an additional way to deal with the difficulty of holding the attention of the congregation is by frequent recaps of what has been said, so that those whose attention has wandered may come back into the sermon—a practice that can also be overdone, in which case it adds to the tediousness that it seeks to avoid.

The length of the average sermon, combined with the frequency of preaching, also has implications for the preparation of a sermon. One reason why few Hispanic preachers write the text of the sermon they are to deliver to their congregation is simply that there is not sufficient time to do so. While a typical Anglo pastor in a mainline denominational would have to write six to eight pages a week, a typical Hispanic pastor would have to write more than forty. Even though the sermon is the center of worship in most Latino churches, the pastors of those churches have many other responsibilities besides preaching, and would find it absolutely impossible to write out all their sermons before they are preached. Most Hispanic pastors have other employment on which they must rely for a significant portion of their income—what in more sophisticated circles are called "tent-making" or "non-stipendiary" ministers. Thus, the reluctance to write the text for a sermon is based not only on theoretical grounds, but also on mere impracticality. (An odd consequence of this situation, and one that is reflected in this book, is that Latina and Latino preachers tend to write out the texts of their sermons only when they are to be preached in English, mostly to non-Hispanic congregations, and within the scope of twenty to twenty-five minutes. Although there are some collections of sermons in Spanish, preached to Hispanic congregations,[2] many of these were written *after* they were preached, on the basis of recollection, and upon request for publication.) In actual practice, most Hispanic preachers work from an outline rather than from a written text—even though many of them have rehearsed in their minds the exact words they hope to use, at least for some crucial points in the sermon.

Naturally, this semi-extemporaneous character of Hispanic preaching contributes to its dialogical character, in which the preacher, even though no one else actually speaks, is in conversation with the congregation, and adjusts the sermon accordingly.

Preaching in a Bicultural Setting

As stated above, the Latino community in this country is itself bilingual and bicultural in varying degrees. While some are English-dominant, others are Spanish-dominant, and many have difficulty determining which is their primary language. In most Latino congregations, people are present from each of these groups. Often, although not always, the various degrees of acculturation into the North American environment also represent different generations—the older generation being the less acculturated, and the younger the most adapted to the dominant culture.

In such a situation, effective preaching must always have bicultural and bilingual dimensions. According to their varying situations and abilities, Hispanic preachers and congregations respond to this need in different ways. In what appears to be the majority of churches, services are held primarily in Spanish, and this is also the case with the sermon; but in such churches it is also common to have some singing in English, and some preachers will throw in at least a few phrases or expressions in that language. At the other extreme, there are Hispanic churches where the dominant language is English. Often in these churches some of the old favorite hymns are sung in Spanish. In a growing number of churches, the actual practice is between these two extremes, and involves more conscious and planned bilingualism. Some congregations hold two services, both bilingual, but one with more English than Spanish, and the other the reverse. Many preachers preach in one language and summarize their sermon in the other. Some translate their own sermon as they go along. An increasing number are becoming adept at a style of preaching in which a few sentences are said in English, the next few in Spanish, and so on, and this is done in such a way that people who have very limited proficiency in one of the two languages can still follow the sermon.

While this biculturalism is most evident within Latino congregations themselves, it is also a factor in any sermon by a Hispanic preacher. Indeed, when one of us stands at the pulpit in a congregation where the majority belongs to the dominant culture, a bicultural situation already exists—except that in this case the divide is not within the congregation, but rather between the congregation and the preacher. Our very presence represents a bicultural and bilingual word. Naturally, in such cases we adapt to the needs of the congregation by speaking in English; but our accent, our name, and our culture cannot be ignored. As has been shown in chapters 2 and 3, our different cultural experiences and perspectives lead us to a somewhat different theological stance and hermeneutics. This, however, should not be seen as a difficulty, but rather as an asset that enriches the church at large. It is on this basis that most Latino and Latina preachers, rather than seeking to leave aside their Hispanic identity when facing a non-Hispanic congregation, use it as a hermeneutical tool and perhaps even as a living illustration of the scope and challenge of the gospel.

At this point, as a final word on bilingualism, it is important that we look at it not as a difficulty that must be overcome, but rather as an instance of the "subversive eschatology" of which I spoke in chapter 2. Certainly the presence of more than one language and culture in a congregation creates difficulties; things are much easier where everyone speaks the same language. Yet, we know that the future to which the church looks forward is a future that includes a great multitude from every nation, tribe, people, and language (Rev. 7:9). Therefore, whenever the church finds ways to worship and to live in multicultural and multilingual ways, it is serving as a subversive sign of the future that it proclaims.

Class, Gender, and Status in the *Púlpito*

When it comes to occupying the *púlpito*, in most Latino churches the distinction between clergy and laity is less marked than in those of the dominant culture. In Roman Catholicism, as was already mentioned, much of traditional popular piety revolves around lay-led rites. These were even more important before the Second Vatican Council, when the Mass was always said in Latin and there seldom was any preaching in it. Since the viability of these rites, especially in situations of great scarcity of priests, depends precisely on their lay leadership, there is an entire sector of the Latino Catholic Church that is quite accustomed to lay leadership, and for which priestly leadership is an added layer above an underlying tradition of lay leadership. For another, more conservative sector of Latino Catholicism, for which the Mass is still the all-important worship event, this only precludes laity from presiding over the sacrament, and usually from preaching in the Mass itself; but this leaves the field wide open for laity to take leadership in "less important" functions—including some forms of preaching. Significantly, in recent years in the Latino Catholic Church a wide array of programs have appeared, usually billed as training for "lay ministries," and many of these programs include courses that are very similar to Protestant classes on homiletics.

For Hispanic Protestants, the distinction between clergy and laity at the *púlpito* is blurred by the practice of *testimonios*. These are a common part of the worship service of most Pentecostal churches, and are becoming increasingly common in "mainline" Protestant churches. A *testimonio*—literally, "witness"—is a brief speech in which believers express what God has done for them. Some speak of their conversion, and the new life they have received from God. Others refer to prayers that have been answered. At their best, they center on God and God's action, and therefore are tantamount to a contextualized proclamation of the gospel.

Since it is quite common to have several such *testimonios* in a single worship service, often by the time the official preacher comes to the *púlpito*, several laypeople have already occupied it. Since many *testimonios* actually begin with a scriptural passage, and they all normally contain references to Scripture, the distinction between *testimonio* and sermon is blurred, to the point that in actual practice the *testimonio* becomes for many a rehearsal for the time when they will become preachers. (It is also customary to invite laity to prepare and to lead the worship service. This they do from the pulpit, which also contributes to the demystification of the *púlpito*.)

Other practices work in the same direction. Many churches have a "youth week" or a "week of the laity," in which young people and laypeople actually preach. Above all, however, what most empowers the laity for preaching is their involvement in evangelism. One of the most common forms of evangelism in Hispanic Protestant churches is the *culto de barrio*—barrio services—where neighbors are invited to a service at a believer's home. Since often there are several such *cultos de barrio* taking place at the same time, preaching in them is entrusted to laity. This in turn produces a cadre of laymen and laywomen who feel called to preach. Significantly, a common experience when seminaries and other such institutions offer programs for the laity is that among the most popular courses are those on preaching. Preaching is seen as a proper function, not only for those called to ordained ministry, but also for laity.

One practical consequence of this is that the preacher—especially the Protestant preacher—must come to the *púlpito* with an authority other than that conferred by ordination or by ecclesiastical appointment. Even the Roman Catholic priest must ground his authority on something other than his ordination, no matter how theologically important this may be for him, because there is a strong anti-clerical strand in Latino cultures and traditions. Indeed, the figure of the priest in much Latin American literature and folklore does not command much respect. In consequence, the mere fact that one stands at the *púlpito* does not confer a Latino or Latina preacher any particular authority. Congregations that listen to several *testimonios* a week soon learn that not all that is said from the pulpit must be accepted as equally authoritative. For many such congregations, there are two important signs of a preacher's authority: wisdom and Scripture.

The wisdom that such Hispanic congregations seek in their preachers may include knowledge, but goes far beyond it. While knowledge is widely respected—especially knowledge of the Bible and related fields—it is also suspect if it is not clearly accompanied and even governed by wisdom. What is more, the excessive reliance on knowledge on the part of some seminary-trained preachers is the main source of suspicion in Latino churches against higher theological education in general, and against seminaries in particular. What outside observers often interpret as an anti-intellectual attitude is quite often in reality a cry for wisdom above knowledge.

Wisdom thus understood is a combination of common sense with personal integrity, vision, sensitivity, seriousness of purpose, and even humor. It certainly requires at least a measure of knowledge, but knowledge that is kept subject to the other elements of wisdom and to the greater goals of the community. It is also wisdom that allows the preacher to listen to the congregation and to be in dialogue with it even while preaching. In fact, one could even say that Hispanic congregations react to knowledge as they would to a performance, while wisdom is the very essence of a true sermon—of the sermon as communal event.

The other source of authority for the Hispanic preacher is Scripture. Again, this authority is particularly necessary because Latino congregations

seldom give their preachers authority on the basis of education, ordination, or appointment. It is for this reason—as well as because that was
what we were taught—that Hispanic preaching has always had a strong
biblical content. In more traditional preaching, this means
that the preacher builds an argument by threading a series of proof texts,
often citing chapter and verse—sometimes to the point that almost every
sentence ends with a reference to the book, chapter, and verse that supposedly prove what one says. This is what chapter 11 calls the "refer-
ence/concordance sermon."

The best Hispanic preaching, however, relies on Scripture in a different way. It does not go to the Sacred Book as to a quarry for proof-texts,
but rather deals seriously with an entire pericope, asking it to interpret
the situation and the calling both of the preacher and congregation. It is
this sort of preaching that is grounded in the hermeneutics discussed in
chapter 13, and which therefore can offer, not only to Hispanics, but also
to the church at large, a renewed appreciation for Scripture and its rele-
vance for today. Clearly, this is not to say that all good Hispanic preaching is expository; narrative, too, is a valid and valuable hermeneutical
and homiletic tool.

If the status of being ordained works differently in Latino churches
than in others, the same is true of class and gender.

In Hispanic congregations, as in all congregations in this country, there
is a measure of class stratification; but this is much less than what is found
in Anglo congregations. In some Hispanic churches there are no persons
of the upper classes, mostly because such persons are rather scarce in the
Hispanic community itself. Beyond that, however, one can say that most
churches are a fairly accurate cross section of the community. Usually,
most of our members are poor, because that is who our people are; but in
practically every congregation there are also persons of higher economic
and social standing. The same is true of levels of education, for our congregations quite often include persons who are illiterate and who sit next
to university professors. One reason for this is that many of these highly
educated persons themselves come from the lower classes, and feel that at
least in part their success is due to the church. Therefore, as they move up
in the social pyramid, many feel that it would be highly ungrateful to leave
the church that supported them in their earlier struggles, and pointed the
way to their success. Another reason is that, since many of these people
are among the first in their families to attain such a level of education, if
they are to continue worshiping with their families they must come to a

church that includes people of various levels of education. Finally, a third reason may be that Hispanic worship tends to allow more room for the emotional and the aesthetic than does the more traditional Anglo worship, which tends to center almost exclusively on the understanding. If the service consists mostly of words and ideas, then either those who have less education will not be able to participate, or those who have more will declare it simplistic and irrelevant. If, on the other hand, it appeals not only to the intellect, but also to the emotions and to the senses, then overcoming differences in levels of education becomes much easier.

The net result of all of this, as far as our subject here is concerned, is that those who stand at the *púlpito* do not necessarily need a level of education that is comparable to the most educated in their congregation. They certainly do need the wisdom that gives them the authority to preach. They need the wisdom to serve as pastors to people involved in situations and activities that they themselves may not be able to understand. That wisdom should also guide them to understand and accept the fact that they need to take into account the knowledge that others may have and they lack. They need knowledge in order to be able to interpret and to proclaim Scripture faithfully—hence the need for theological education at all levels. But as I visit Latino congregations throughout the nation I find hundreds of highly respected—and also highly wise and intelligent—preachers whose level of education is far below that of a goodly number of their parishioners—and yet these parishioners respect them and find in their preaching the word of God for their lives. Since elsewhere I have compared the Latino church with an extended family,[3] one could say that this means that in that church class differences tend to diminish, and that the authority of its leaders has to do more with their wisdom and their ability to connect what they say with the gospel than with any outside validation—just as authority within an extended family is granted to those whose wisdom is proved over the years.

Issues of gender also impinge on the Hispanic *púlpito*. They impinge first of all because we are heirs to a culture that has very definite, and often quite oppressive, gender roles. This has been made worse by outside influences that have sought to ground these differences—as well as others brought by the missionaries—on the Bible and the will of God. Fortunately, the sort of preacher on whom we are centering our attention in this book is usually far beyond debates regarding the leadership of women in the church and society, the ordination of women, and the like. Indeed, in the Latino community women preachers have taken the lead, not only on the issues that could be labeled as specifically "women's issues," but also on all the other issues raised in this book. As the samples that follow will amply demonstrate, women preachers are among the most creative in the Hispanic community.

One point at which issues of gender must still be debated and new solutions found in the Hispanic community has to do with language and gender. Some of the solutions applied in English work in Spanish. For instance, just as we have learned not to refer in English to humankind as "man," so have we learned not to speak of *el hombre* as if this were a generic term. In a few cases, solutions are simpler in Spanish than in English. For instance, the possessive *su* means "his" as well as "her" and "its," and therefore we can refer to the people of God as *su pueblo* without thereby implying that God is male, as the English "his people" does. But in spite of these few instances the fact remains that issues of grammatical gender are much more complicated in Spanish than in English.

Part of the difficulty is that, while in English grammatical gender is used only in conjunction with sex (father, mother, niece, nephew, aunt, uncle, sister, brother, and so on), in Spanish every noun has a gender, and this does not always reflect the sex of the signified. For instance, the word *persona* is feminine and has no masculine counterpart. Therefore whenever one refers to someone as a "person" one uses feminine articles and adjectives, regardless of the person's physical gender. On the other hand, *individuo* is masculine, and therefore when speaking of a woman as an *individuo* one must use masculine grammatical forms.

This use of gender controlled by grammar rather than by sex is such that in Spanish we often use words that cannot be translated into English, such as *femenino* and *masculina*—the masculine form of the word "feminine" and the feminine form of the word "masculine." We do this without even thinking when we say, for instance, that "«libreta» es un término *femenino*, mientras que «libro» es una palabra *masculina*."

(On the positive side, one might add that, although *Dios* is masculine, *Trinidad* and *Providencia* are feminine, and so is *Divinidad*. Therefore, one can easily find ways to refer to the Deity in both feminine and masculine language. Indeed, one does this quite often without even thinking about it.)

What further complicates matters is that in Spanish not only nouns have genders, but also so do articles and adjectives, and they must agree with the gender of the noun. Therefore, if one wished to avoid all gender-specific language, most phrases would have to be spoken twice, once in one gender and then in the other. For instance, "the good Christian men and women" would become "los buenos hombres cristianos y las buenas mujeres cristianas." Obviously, this rapidly becomes unmanageable.

Finally, the complexities of grammatical gender in Spanish are such that grammarians distinguish, not two nor even three, but *five* different genders![4]

All of this is not to say that issues of language are not important. On the contrary, they are of the greatest importance, particularly since words are the main medium of communication from the *púlpito*. (We say "the main medium," because for us gestures are also an important and even a necessary means of communication. However, that is a subject for another essay.) One of the reasons that it is difficult or even impossible to find grammatical solutions to issues of gender exclusion and injustice is that the grammar itself, as all of language and of society, has been deeply affected by traditional practices of exclusion. This makes the task even more important and urgent, even though it will take generations of linguistic exploration to find adequate solutions to some of our problems.

Meanwhile, Latino and Latina preachers attempt to improve their language with reference to gender by several means. First of all, in those cases where they work, we use the same procedures as we do in English. Second, even though we cannot do it constantly, in those cases where it most matters we must make a special effort to use inclusive language. Thus, for instance, we speak of "el pastor o la pastora," or "la predicadora o el predicador," even though we cannot at every turn say "el cristiano o la cristiana." Third, in the examples we use, precisely because we must refer to a specific gender, we try to break stereotypes. For instance, we cannot speak of a generic "the doctor"; we must say either "el doctor" or "la doctora"; in such cases we tend to opt for the latter. Finally, sometimes Hispanic preachers will speak for a few minutes in the feminine form, referring to "la cristiana," and then switch to the masculine "el cristiano." Obviously, the danger in this procedure is that, given the stereotypes that circulate in our culture, our hearers might hear one paragraph as referring exclusively to female Christians, and the other as referring only to males.

Conclusion

With so many issues and realities impinging on it, one could well say that the *púlpito* is a crowded place to stand! Perhaps that is one of the reasons why so many of us, when we preach, move in and out of the pulpit!

It is crowded! It is uncomfortable! It is insecure! It is even threatening! To stand at the *púlpito* is a difficult task and an awesome responsibility— made particularly awesome by the claim and the hope that somehow God's word speaks through our often ill-chosen words.

When thus described, to stand at the *púlpito* is an impossible task. Yet it is an impossible task made possible by the grace of God. Therefore, the very fact that we dare stand at the crowded, insecure, and threatening *púlpito* is in itself a witness to the grace of God that we preach, and with-out which we would not dare preach!

Notes

1. See chapter 1, n. 28.
2. See chapter 1, n. 37.
3. See chapter 2, n. 5.
4. Besides the obvious *masculino* and *femenino* (since *género* is a masculine word, the name of the gender takes a masculine form: *femenino*), there is the *neutro*, the *epiceno*, and the *ambiguo*. The *género neutro* usually refers to abstractions such as *lo bueno* and *lo malo*. The *género epiceno*, while employing either a masculine or a feminine form, requires an adjective to specify gender, and in that case the adjective can be either masculine or feminine, no matter what the form of the noun may be—*la ballena hembra, la ballena macho*. Finally, some nouns have *género ambiguo*, and can take either masculine or feminine articles and adjectives—*el mar bravío* or *la mar bravía*. To further complicate matters, some-times euphony requires the use of a masculine article where a feminine form would otherwise be employed—*el águila mexicana*.

PART II

At the Púlpito

Hispanic Homiletic Practice

CHAPTER FIVE

CHILD OF GOD

(Luke 1:57-66)

Minerva G. Carcaño

Minerva G. Carcaño is a United Methodist bishop, elected to the episcopate July 2004. This sermon was originally preached at the Third United Methodist Global Gathering in Kansas City, held April 10-13, 1997. It calls attention to the plight of suffering children in the world. The sermon seeks to encourage the audience to care for children, who are sacred before God. Its main topic is that each creature is a child of God. In this sense, the sermon exemplifies how Hispanics address social justice issues from a biblical perspective.

What a different view of John the Baptist! Rather than the prophet of sin and repentance breathing down our necks, we get to see him as a gentle baby being born, circumcised, and named. John is a true blessing to his parents and to his extended community. His birth is indeed a miracle of great significance.

Father Abraham and mother Sarah had seen the grace of God in their old age and birthed a child. So had Hannah and Elkanah. But who would think that God would bless Zechariah and Elizabeth in that same way—not even Zechariah believed!

Zechariah was a man of faith: an elder; a priest, in fact. He was a man of status and wisdom who knew the great stories of faith, enough so that he remembers Abraham's story when he praises God after the naming of his son and the recovery of his voice. Yet, Zechariah did not initially believe that the day of the birth of his son would come. That, as John's name signifies, the day of God's favor would arrive.

I can understand Zechariah's doubting. As I was preparing this sermon it occurred to me that an average life span in Zechariah and Elizabeth's time was about half of what it is today, and suddenly I could identify with him perfectly. My husband, Thomas, and I had our only child when he was forty and I was thirty-seven. When we showed up for the birthing classes at our local hospital the other pregnant parents called us "Sir" and "Ma'am," gave us the best seats in the room, and worried about us when we had to do the required floor exercises. It was then that I decided I was not above using a little hair color on my hair, and Thomas shaved off his graying beard. It was an exciting time in our lives—also embarrassing, frightening, and often just unbelievable. But how we wanted that child! Zechariah and Elizabeth in their old age and through their travails desperately wanted their child. And they handled their situation as best they could.

Elizabeth spent her pregnancy in seclusion and Zechariah spent his pregnant months deaf and dumb because he did not believe the announcement of the angel Gabriel. The truth of the matter is that neither one of them yet knew the full meaning of the life of this child they had conceived. Elizabeth thought the child she carried in her womb was one who would simply erase the disgrace she had so long endured among her people for being barren, and nothing more. Zechariah was disturbed to the point of deafness and muteness in the very thought that God was mindful of him and his wife, and nothing more. Both Elizabeth and Zechariah needed time to consider this child of theirs.

Wouldn't it be wonderful if somehow every couple, every home, every extended family, every neighborhood, every barrio, every village, every city and town, every province and nation where a child is being expected would stop and consider that child.

I wonder whether if we prayerfully considered the children being born to us in this country, we would allow 2,660 babies to be born each day into poverty. Whether we would neglect those babies so that every day three of them would die and on those same days, six more of them as children and teens would commit suicide. Whether we would be so careless with those children's lives that we would place firearms in their hands and watch as they kill each other off, fifteen a day. Or whether we would stand for the abuse or neglect of yet another 8,493 children every day of the year, in this country.

If we prayerfully considered every child being born in this world on this night, would we allow children to go begging on the streets of Mexico City; bombs to be dropped on the children living in Bosnia, Zaire, Cambodia, and Israel? Would we stand for the sexual mutilation of little girls in Egypt and Nigeria or the swollen bellies of malnourished children in Rwanda? Would we be complacent as Indian children's little hands and beautiful eyes are ruined while they make rugs for our floors and soccer balls for our games?

Elizabeth and Zechariah considered their child and came to know that he was a gift from God, named by God. And when the time came to take their baby to the temple for circumcision and naming, Elizabeth and Zechariah went in the full knowledge that the child they held so closely and so dearly in their arms was nothing less than God's grace for them and for all those around them. They went confident that they knew who this child was and what he meant to them.

And so when the priests in the temple were about to name Zechariah and Elizabeth's child by giving him his father's name, Elizabeth spoke up and said, "No! He is to be called John." And when those same priests chose to ignore Elizabeth, as was their custom, and inquired what the good father would want his son named, Zechariah to their surprise concurred with Elizabeth writing on a tablet very clearly, "*His name is John.*" It was not, "His name shall be John," or "His mother and I have decided that his name will be John," or, "I as his father have decided that his name will be John." The matter was not open for discussion. The decision had already been made. This was heaven's child, and heaven had chosen his name: "His name *is* John!" His name is the grace of God. In essence Elizabeth and Zechariah gave witness to the fact that the child they were presenting was not their child. He was God's child.

What will it take for us to recognize that the children of our time, not unlike that baby in Elizabeth and Zechariah's arms, are God's children? Perhaps it's going to take acquiring anew the clarity of relationship that children themselves possess. We adults know all the right words, but children know what the words mean.

One Sunday morning while serving as the pastor of a church I invited all the children to come forward to assist me with a baptism. We were baptizing a baby boy who had almost died at birth. Before calling the parents of the baby to be baptized, I explained to the children that through baptism we were receiving a new member into our family. The child we were about to baptize was a new baby brother sent from God for all of us and we should love him and care for him. "When I call the parents of our new baby brother to bring him forward so that we can baptize him, let's gather close so that he can feel our love," I said to those children.

So I called the parents forward and they came with this miracle of a child, and the children all squished in tight and I began to lead the congregation in the baptismal ritual. Then I took the baby in my left arm, asked for his name, and dipped my right hand in the water of the baptismal font preparing to baptize him. But then something happened that had never happened to me in all my twenty years of ministry. When I turned to place my hand on the baby's head another hand was already there. It was a tiny little hand and as I looked over my left shoulder I saw whom it belonged to. A child only 2 years older than the baby I was holding had been lifted up by her father so that she could see this baby, and she had taken my words very seriously and had reached out to touch this baby and show him her love. Her little eyes were closed in an attitude of prayer. For a second my ego got the best of me when I hesitated to see if that child would move her hand. But then something stirred in my spirit and I placed my hand over hers and we baptized that baby together. That two-year-old child made my words real—this was God's child we were baptizing, a baby brother full of God's grace, worthy of all the love we could possibly give him. It was a beautiful, uninhibited, public moment of loving affirmation and connectedness.

It was precisely at the moment that Zechariah was able to acknowledge publicly that the child he and Elizabeth had birthed was God's child, that Zechariah's "mouth was opened and his tongue freed, and he began to speak, praising God" and prophesying. It is impossible to truly speak when we don't believe what we are called to say, but oh so impossible to be silent when we do believe!

I am in a mentoring relationship with four twelve-year-old Hispanic girls from a middle school in the community where I live and serve. One of the public comments that these girls have made about their lives is that their parents never speak to them, or they speak to them only, according to them, to scold them or tell them what to do. When I heard this it made me stop in my tracks and think about my relationship with my own daughter. I had to confess that on some days my communication with her leans heavily on the side of scolding and bossing. Not enough listening and communicating. I found it extremely interesting that these girls, contrary to what I had thought, wanted *more* communication, more relationship with their parents and other adults in their lives rather than less. They yearn to hear a word of affirmation and support—a good word. What better word to say to these girls, to my daughter, to your children, and to all the children and young people in this world, "See what love the Father has given [you], that [you] should be called children of God; and that is what [you] are" (1 John 3:1). *The problem is, though, that if we say that, we'd better mean it.*

Unfortunately, in the U.S.A., I don't think we mean it and so we find ourselves deaf and mute like Zechariah before his moment of faith, unable to hear our children and even more, unable to speak a relevant word to them. Check our situation with me:

- We say we love children yet we accept homelessness for thousands of children across this nation;
- We say we care about children yet our child poverty rate is among the highest in the developed world;
- We say we defend the rights of children yet every day U.S.-born children are deported, thrown out of this country to insecure places because of the immigration status of their parents;
- We say children are the most precious thing in our lives, yet every night we allow fast-food restaurants to use them as cheap labor;
- We say children are the most important members of our nation, yet every night we allow 100,000 of them to walk our streets in prostitution;
- We say children are the priority in our society, yet mothers have to fight for maternity leave to nurse and nurture those children in those critical first months of life, and paternity leave is almost unheard of.

Is it any different in the rest of the world?

No wonder we find it difficult to speak honestly and openly, even when we are called to say something as true as "You, our children, are the sacred sons and daughters of God—placed in our hands for tender and faithful care."

Some of you may be getting comfortable in your seats right about now, thinking, "I don't have any kids," or "I've done all right by my children."

Well, let me remind you that God's household includes all of God's children and if you live in that household, then they're all yours and they're all mine. It's a thought worth pondering.

Zechariah and Elizabeth's family and neighbors pondered what they heard about the newest member of their community. His name is John—God's showing of favor. If this is his name, we ask, "What then will this child become?"

God, of course, chose John for a very special mission. He was to become a prophet and a teacher. He taught persons the way of God and became the most excellent prophet—the last and the clearest prophet of the old covenant *and* the prophet of the new covenant. He was to become the forerunner of the Messiah himself and excelled so in ministry that only Jesus the Christ surpassed him. He was the pastor in God's hands who dramatically and decisively turned persons' hearts from sinfulness to the faithful following of the Lord Jesus. He was called and anointed to be an instrument of God's mercy. John is to be the morning star, the dayspring from on high, and the lamp that burns itself out in giving light and is put away only when the sun rises (Luke 1:78, 5:35). John was something! But isn't every child of God something? Somebody?

I hear the voice of the Prophet Isaiah as he catches a glimpse of the coming peaceful kingdom of God, and says, "A little child shall lead...." (Isa. 11:6). And wasn't it Jesus who said, "Let the little children come to me, and do not stop them; for it is to such as these that the kingdom of heaven belongs" (Matt. 19:14)? And was the Apostle Paul right when he wrote that God's children are destined for glory through the work of Jesus the Christ (Rom. 8:21)? Yes! Of course Paul was right! And who among us would question Jesus? And in retrospect, we know that Isaiah was always on the mark.

But, how do the children know? How did John know that he was destined for great things? You and I instinctively know how it happened.

Elizabeth cradled him in her arms and told him the story of his birth with great love. Zechariah took him on his knee often and sang to him his great prophetic song over and over again saying to him with pride: "Son, that song is talking about you!" And John's aunts and uncles, his cousins and friends and all his neighbors told him about the marvelous day of his birth, the incredible day of his naming, and the great person he would become in God's hands.

Do you think any of these persons let John go hungry or homeless? Do you think they neglected him? Do you think they ever worked him like an animal of burden? Do you think they emotionally or sexually abused him? Do you think they ever beat him? I suspect that they followed the discipline of Proverbs; but beat him till he was black and blue, broken inside, and trembling in horror? I think not. How could they ever conceive of doing any of these things to John when they knew he was a child of God?

So why do so many of our children go hungry and homeless, are worked to the bone, are abused emotionally and sexually, and beaten to death? Could it be that we have forgotten their name? Forgotten that God has named them calling them son, daughter, child of mine? Fortunately there are some out there who remember the name of the children, and children themselves are giving witness of them.

Lauralee is now a student at Harvard, but for most of her life she was a homeless child. She recalls a day from her years of homelessness: "My feet hurt from walking all day. My mouth was dry from not getting enough to eat or drink. All I wanted to do was go home and rest. But there was no home to go to." She was nine years old.

One day she met a middle-aged Palestinian man who was also homeless who told her about God. He taught her that homeless people are not defined by their homelessness and that she belonged to something and someone other than a shelter. What she learned from that man changed her life, and now Lauralee prepares to be all that she can be. "But I'm not completely unburdened," she says; "I occasionally feel myself struggling to hold on to my identity at Harvard, where wealth and power are so often taken for granted."

I know a young man from Honduras with a huge heart and a great big vision. Oscar grew up in extreme poverty, the eldest child in a broken home.

- At 11, the defender and protector of his mother and five
  siblings;
- At 14, a broken-down immigrant;
- At 18, a street-wise inmate in a penitentiary.

But somewhere along his life's journey someone cared about Oscar. It was a pastor. "You are God's creation, Oscar," she had said, "precious to your Maker. God loves you and will always be with you." Those words and the loving care that came with them were what saved Oscar's life. I met Oscar four years ago, a blessing to my life. He wrote to me recently and said that God has placed a vision in his heart. He is going to establish and direct a home for women and children who are victims of abuse in Honduras. He doesn't know how he's going to do it, but he knows that God will be with him. Did I have any ideas on how he could fulfill God's calling in his life? He was open to any help he could get.

On the outskirts of Albuquerque, New Mexico, lives a young girl named Mayra. One cold winter morning Mayra accompanied her mother to a church as she looked for work. There was no work to be had at the church, but the church members gave them food and coats, and fixed their home so that it would be warm, and invited them to church. Her mother hesitated about going to church; but Mayra went joyfully—she liked these people. Through this experience Mayra met Christ. She was seven years old. She is now twelve and has led her mother and her younger brothers and sister to Christ. She's still working on her father. "I know God is going to do something special with my life—I just feel it," she proclaims, as tears of joy run down her cheeks.

Children: Wonderful, incredible, amazing children. John, Lauralee, Oscar, Mayra—but what's in a name? *Everything*, if that name happens to be *Child of God*.

CHAPTER SIX

TRUE WORSHIP

(Isaiah 1:1-2, 10-20; Psalm 50:1-8, 22-23; Hebrews
11:1-16; Luke 12:32-40)

Elizabeth Conde-Frazier

*Elizabeth Conde-Frazier, who is Assistant Professor of Religious
Education at Claremont School of Theology, is a Baptist minister
with extensive pastoral experience. She recently has published a
book entitled* A Many Colored Kingdom: Multicultural
Dynamics for Spiritual Formation *(Grand Rapids: Baker
Academic, 2004), with S. Steve Kang and Gary A. Parrett.*

*This sermon was preached originally at an Anglo-European
Baptist Church that invited Conde-Frazier because they wanted to
be exposed to a Latina pastor and scholar. The sermon addresses the
lectionary readings for that particular day. Its topic is worship,
viewed from the particular perspective of a Latina minister.*

Introduction

When my children were between the ages of four and eight years old,
they often showered my husband and me with spontaneous expressions of
love. They would pick flowers in the field and tell us how much they
loved us as they handed them to us. Other times they would make up
songs that told of their love and their reasons for their love, or the song

would speak of how wonderful we were and what we did for them. As they learned to write poetry, their expressions took that form. And, of course, there is the artwork. Later they dedicated songs on the piano to us. What wonderful expressions!

Maturing Expressions of Love

As they have grown older, their expressions continue, except that they have matured. In more recent years, both my husband and I have been engaged in doctoral studies. The children expressed their love by supporting us in their prayers and by helping out around the house. They have played a bit more quietly if we were writing at the computer; or they gave us neck and shoulder massages and wrote notes of encouragement to us.

But then there are the expressions of love that go beyond us. There are values that we strive to live by, and their expressions of love for us are to exemplify those values. Those values go beyond the family and become guides for being citizens of the world. We become involved in writing a letter to the president, a representative, or a senator on an issue of justice and peace. We go to a farm and pick vegetables all day for the hungry. They take risks at school and take both a stance and action against discrimination. These too are expressions of love to us as their parents, even though they are directed toward others.

What Is Worship?

So, what is worship? Is it not our expression to God of our love? To worship then, we must believe that God exists, that God loves us. We need a story that confirms that God has loved and continues to love us. Our story is a confirmation of the biblical story. Our worship then speaks of who God is and why we love God—it's an articulation of our faith. It is a variety of our expressions of love toward God.

Our Order of Worship: One Form

Worship takes a form, as seen this morning in our order of worship. There are songs whose words are arranged in poetic fashion. There are prayers that tell God what is in our hearts. And there is music dedicated to God. There is a time to hear God speak to us, as well. Love is listening to the other. We learn more about God that our love may grow, that our expressions of love may mature. That happens through the Scriptures and the sermon and teachings.

Then there are expressions of love that exemplify that we are citizens of the reign of God, of a new order in the world. We express interest, concern, and caring for each other. This is done sharing our celebrations and concerns, and the intercessory prayer. This is done in the offertory. The offerings were given to please God; they provided for the priests who did not receive land as the others did, because their job was to look after the things of the temple. The offerings were also to make provision for the poor. The proportion was 10 percent. In the Latino church, tithing is taken very seriously.

In other words, the tithe is an expression of love to God. What shall I render to the Lord for all God's bounty for me? It is also an expression of loving my neighbor as myself, for if we do it for one of these little ones we have done it unto the Lord. "You shall love the Lord your God with all of your heart and all of your mind and all of your strength and your neighbor as yourself." When I'm in need, I would like someone to give not just what was left over in their pocket, an afterthought, but I would like them to give a particular portion set out because they had me in mind and, therefore, in heart.

Last, in your order of worship I see a hymn of processing into the world. Your worship goes on beyond this place. It continues as you leave here. We continue to worship through how we live our everyday lives.

Isaiah: God's Judgment

Now, after having said all this, can you imagine if in the midst of a special worship service of the year, not during the summer, but Easter or Christmas, and the sanctuary is decorated, all the liturgical symbols are present, the order of worship had been handled with great detail, the choir sang majestically, and the organ and piano were resounding in grand fashion, so that you could feel the tremor of the music in your chest. Everyone participating wore well-coordinated robes in rich colors; the flowers filled the air with their scent and beauty, and there was a sense of awe of the divine. And then, a guest speaker came forth, and instead of words of rejoicing and comfort, the speaker uttered words of judgment and said that all of your display of worship was nothing but a hollow mockery to God, and said that God was not pleased at all but was angry and appalled because you were insensitive and full of lust, because your hearts were hardened to God and neighbor. You would say this guest speaker was "wacked" and would escort him or her out; or you would walk out yourselves in anger and disappointment and perhaps disgust. How dare this person come in here and say such things—ruin the worship! Everything was so perfect and then they spoiled it. Who does this person think he or she is? Reverend Varney, I'm sure, would try to salvage the moment in some sort of a way.

But, this is exactly what Isaiah did in the passage we just read. He interrupted worship with a message of judgment that no one wanted to hear. What is a message of judgment all about anyway? God's judgment is the expression of concern of a loving parent who fears that he or she has lost the children because they have cut themselves off from the values taught, and from the things that identify them together as being part of each other, part of the family. This creates a distance unlike geographic distance. It means not having something in common, no words or purpose, and no meaning to share. The activities of life of one and the other seem futile to each other. There is no spark, no energy, no interest, no conversation, and no bond. Their covenant has been broken.

The prophet shows us the yearning heart of a hurting and pleading parent. "I reared children and brought them up, but they rebelled against me." The people have gone so far from what God intends in the world that they are against God. This is the spirit of the words of judgment. It is more of an urging, a warning. It says: "Look! This is what happens when you take such actions. If you are unjust it will produce violence against yourselves. It is inevitable!" In verses 18-19 the announcement and warning of the consequences to come are once more padded with the yearning love of a parent who says: "But this doesn't have to be this way. Come, let us argue it out, let us reason together. Even if what you have already done is terrible—though your sins are like scarlet—we can still fix this; they shall be like snow. If, if, if you are willing, willing and obedient—if you repent, if you take a look at what you have done and decide that indeed this is not what you want and your desire is to change instead, to take other action that begins to correct the relationships you have with others—to bring justice! Then you will eat the good of the land—then the good things you do will produce fruit. But, if you refuse and rebel, then you shall be devoured by the sword—you shall live as victims of continuing violence and it shall destroy you."

A Deeper Understanding of Worship

The prophet's words not only invite us but also urge us greatly to deepen our understanding of worship. This religious impulse—if we can call it that—is being wasted, it is meaningless unless we covenant, make a commitment of ourselves to the service of God. Where do we begin? In the letter to the Romans, Paul says: "I appeal to you therefore, brothers and sisters, by the mercies of God, to present your bodies as a living sacrifice, holy and acceptable to God, which is your spiritual worship" (Rom. 12:1). Some versions say "this is your right worship."

This right worship is to turn from our blindness to others. To turn from our not knowing or understanding the journey or reasons for doing things that others have, to understanding, or at least knowing something about their culture and plight. It is to turn from not even knowing that they exist. There are countries we don't teach children about—they can't even find them on the map.

To be healed from blindness is to see the peoples in our own backyards who become statistics or bothers. It is to see them before we meet them in court and we ask for their destruction—this is our spiritual worship. To ask in the PTA meeting why we leave certain things out of the curriculum. To ask why certain people can't afford to live in our neighborhood, asking if this is something wrong, not natural, or if it is an accepted reality. This is our spiritual worship. To turn from our insensitivity, because when we are blind insensitivity follows. In our society we separate ourselves from those with whom God expects us to share. We separate ourselves both physically and philosophically. We reason that people are lazy, there are criminal elements, illegal aliens; they don't deserve what we have; they haven't worked for it. We legislate against them. This causes us to separate ourselves morally, and compassion and mercy cannot flow. We can't imitate God who is merciful and compassionate.

Persons we don't see are not part of our conversations, our decisions and considerations. They are not part of our budget, our time, or what we do with our lives, or our vocations—our work in the world. Liturgy means the work of the people.

The gospel reading guides us to change:

Do not be afraid, little flock, for it is your Father's good pleasure to give you the kingdom. Sell your possessions, and give alms. Make purses for yourselves that do not wear out, an unfailing treasure in heaven, where no thief comes near and no moth destroys. For where your treasure is, there your heart will be also. Be dressed for action. (Luke 12:32-35)

These verses show us how to change our priorities, our worldview, and our logic. The secret is: do not fear. Trust in God counteracts fear. We have the heroes of faith before us from the book of Hebrews, Abel, and Abraham, and Sarah, and I know of some heroes of faith today:

- A woman who gave her down payment for a house to a family whose provider had become ill.
- A church with little knowledge of English that decided to fight for a better education for the children of the neighborhood.
- Another congregation that became a sanctuary for persons coming from El Salvador, running from the horrors of war.
- I know of two pastors who decided to start a partnership between their congregations. The result was young people whose parents had not gone to college now being able to go.

Be not afraid.

Let mutual love continue. Do not neglect to show hospitality to strangers for by doing that some have entertained angels without knowing it. (Heb. 13:2)

Be not afraid.

Remember those who are in prison, as though you were in prison with them; those who are being tortured, as though you yourselves were being tortured. (Heb. 13:3)

Be not afraid.

Keep your lives free from the love of money and be content with what you have; for he has said, "I will never leave you nor forsake you." So that we can say with confidence, "the Lord is my helper." (Heb. 13:5)

I will not be afraid.

Let our worship be the sacrifices of right relationship with one another in society. Our trust, the actions that flow from it, is an offering to God valued in a different currency.

Come, let us reason together, says God. We have been invited, urged, to be willing and obedient with the promise of good. Or, if we rebel, there is a promise of the consequences of violence on our streets. We already see this. To make a difference is our choice today; or to let it devour us is also our choice today. Let us consider the worship which is pleasing to God—the giving of our time, talent and treasures—the offering of our imagination and strength to make a difference as a body and not only as individuals. How do you choose to worship, then?

Let us give strong consideration to this urging from God. When you make budget considerations, in your committee meetings, when you make vocational decisions, and when you ask, "What shall I render for God's benefits to me?" Let us give strong consideration to this urging from God.

SEVEN LAST WORDS

Virgilio Elizondo

> *Virgilio Elizondo is considered a pioneer in the field of Hispanic Theology. A Catholic priest born in Texas, having earned his doctorate in France, Elizondo came back home to lead the Mexican American Catholic Center (MACC) in San Antonio. He is highly regarded worldwide as a leading ethnic theologian.*
>
> *This sermon beautifully exemplifies the deep connection between preaching and worship in the Hispanic community. A sermon for Good Friday, it showcases the central role of the Holy Week celebrations for both Catholic and Protestant Hispanics. In addition, it is a dialogical sermon (originally preached with Patricia Elizondo) that demonstrates that preaching is a lively way of doing "teología en conjunto."*

Song: "Perdona a tu pueblo, Señor"

Narrator: The procurator's soldiers took Jesus inside the prætorium and collected the troops around him, they stripped off his clothes and wrapped him in a scarlet military cloak, and weaving a crown out of thorns they fixed it on his head and stuck a reed in his right hand. Then they began to mock him by dropping to their knees before him saying, "All hail to the king." They also spat at him. Afterwards, they took hold of the reed and kept striking him on the head. Finally, when they had finished making a fool of him, they stripped him of the cloak, dressed him in his own clothes, and led him off to be crucified.

Song: "Camino del Calvario"

Narrator: When they brought Jesus to the site of Golgotha, which means Skull Place, they tried to give him wine drugged with myrrh but he would not take it. There they crucified him.

Song: "Oh Dios, ten Piedad"

Narrator: When they came to the Skull Place as it was called, they crucified him there and the criminals as well, one on his right and the other on his left. Jesus said "Father forgive them for they know not what they do."

Preacher: From the throne of his cathedral Jesus proclaimed God's message. It was a beautiful and powerful word of life. In a world poisoned and torn apart by violence, vengeance, betrayals, abandonment, insults, and indifference, forgiveness is the only way to inner freedom, peace, and tranquility. Holding grudges enslaves and embitters; forgiveness liberates and restores life. Without forgiveness life is worse than death, and death is eternal torment. Jesus was betrayed, abused, and abandoned; yet he lived to forgive and he forgave to the end. For only in forgiveness is even death dissolved into life everlasting and previous pains transformed unto unending joy, and to forgive is to live.

Song: "Perdónanos Nuestras Culpas"

Narrator:	One of the criminals hanging in crucifixion blasphemed him: "Aren't you the Messiah? Then save yourself and us." But the other one rebuked him: "Have you no fear of God? Seeing you are under the same sentence. We deserve it. After all we are only paying the price for what we have done; but this man has done nothing wrong." He then said "Jesus, remember me when you enter upon your reign." Jesus replied, "I assure you this day you will be with me in paradise."
Preacher:	Is there one of us who has not failed in some way or another? Is there one of us who at some time has not been a "criminal" deserving punishment? "I have done nothing wrong," some would say, while others confess: "I deserve it." Denial is as great a curse as unending self-flagellation. Acting as if no wrong had been committed is as great a sickness as a constant torments of guilt. But our unquestioned trust is in the one who dies for us, who rehabilitates everyone. As always, even in dying Jesus has the way to inner healing. Simply admit your guilt, trust in him, and God will do the rest. Today, you shall be with me in paradise.

Song: "El Señor es Tierno y Compasivo"

Narrator:	Seeing his mother there with the disciple whom he loved, Jesus said to his mother, "Woman there is your son." In turn he said to the disciple, "There is your mother." From that hour onward the disciple took her into his home.
Preacher:	No one in this world should ever be left alone or unattended. The best insurance policy, the best orphanage, the best nursing home will not suffice without personal care and tenderness. To be humanly alive we need to be concerned for others and know that others are concerned about us. We need to be loved and to love. Not even death can separate us from those we love, from

those who in life have given us life. Jesus' physical agony on the cross is overcome and transcended by his compassion, by his tender care for those around him. Others can nail his body to the cross; but they cannot pull him back from loving others on earth and beyond. Only in caring for others does our own suffering become submerged in the peacefulness of eternal life—not the life of the hereafter, but the beginning of eternal life which is found in today's bonds of love and concern and care. To love is to live eternally.

Song: "Madre de Nuestro Pueblo"

Narrator: Then toward mid-afternoon, Jesus cried out in a loud tone "Eli, Eli, lama sabacthani?" that is, "My God, my God, why have you forsaken me?"

Preacher: What an incredible love Jesus showed for all of us! For there is no greater love than to share in the deepest agony of the beloved. In his own body and spirit Jesus shared our excruciating pains of embarrassment, of shame, of failure, of alienation, of loneliness, and of distress. Because of his unlimited love for us, God raised him to eternal life. When I feel totally down on the affairs of life I do not fear; I do not despair, for I know that the Son of God is with me to give me hope. In the abandonment of Jesus, I am rescued from my own abandonment. Abandonment never again, for God is with me no matter what.

Song: "Oh Dios, ¿Por Qué Nos Has Abandonado?"

Narrator: After that, realizing that everything was now completed set to fulfill the scripture, Jesus said: "I thirst."

Preacher: Jesus was condemned by his people and abandoned by his friends. The thousands who had wanted to make him king now demanded his death. When all goes well, we have plenty of friends and followers. When we fail, we are quickly betrayed and abandoned. Those who were proud of us quickly become ashamed of us, and even of having known us; those who have received favors quickly throw mud. The loneliness of condemnation, of shame, and abandonment is a worse torment than death itself. The deepest thirst of the human spirit is not for drink, but for understanding, for acceptance, for accompaniment. Only we can offer this drink of life that will quench the deepest thirst of the human heart parched by rejection after abandonment. Only we can give the drink of life.

Song: "Señor, ten Piedad"

Narrator: When Jesus took the wine he said, "Now it is complete."

Preacher: Not the recognition of defeat but the affirmation of triumph, the beautiful satisfaction of the artist, the scientist, the architect, the cook, the janitor, the parent, the teacher, who has worked hard, struggled through the many unsuspected difficulties, suffered the misunderstandings and maybe even ridicule and failure, but has remained faithful in bringing the project to completion. Jesus remained absolutely faithful to God's project for humanity to love others no matter the cost and no matter the response; to love others that all might someday be one. Our task in life is not to win approval or popularity but to love everyone no matter what. All our power and might cannot destroy the force of love. Jesus, in spite of the most scandalous denunciations and gruesome attacks, remained steadfast in the way of love. Others thought he had failed in disgrace; but he shouts a spontaneous cry of gratitude, of triumph, of victory: It is finished. It is finally complete. Death is not the end of life but merely a completion of life's project, which as every great piece of art, continues to live forever.

Song: "Victoria, Tú Reinarás"

Narrator: The curtain in the sanctuary was torn in two, Jesus uttered a loud cry and said, "Father into your hands I commend my spirit."

Preacher: What a beautiful way to depart from this world with complete confidence in the God of life! Even in dying Jesus is introducing us to the tenderness and unending care of the God of life. No matter what life has in store for me, I need never despair; for no matter what, God is with me, and into God's hands I entrust my life and my destiny. What is there left for me to do, my Jesus? Thanks for the profound satisfaction and blissful peacefulness of knowing that I have done my best in living God's will, and God asks nothing more. For God's will is that I might live, that I might live to the fullest. And in seeking to do God's will I come to the fullness of life both here and in eternity. Those who are faithful, ready for God's way of love, even if they should die, need not fear, for they shall live forever.

Song: "Adoramus Te Christe"

Narrator: The centurion who stood guard over him on seeing the manner of his death declared, "Clearly this man was the Son of God."

Song: "Las Bienaventuranzas de la Paz"

Preacher: Oh Lord, in your humanity, help me to see your divinity, and your divinity in the human. Help me find myself, my true self. Help me discover the way, the goal, and to learn that life itself is for only you, and that in you there is fullness of life. Amen.

Song: "Dios y Hombre"

CHAPTER EIGHT

OF FIGS AND GRAPES

(Luke 13:1-9)

Justo L. González

> *This sermon was originally preached at a meeting sponsored by the Florida Conference of The United Methodist Church, in Lakeland, Florida. It was preached in English, to an audience consisting mostly of church leaders from the majority culture. Those planning the event had told the preacher that one of their main concerns was that some people in the area resisted involvement in Hispanic and other minority ministries, claiming that Hispanics and other minorities were in need due to their own failures. Therefore, part of the preacher's agenda was to counteract such opinions, but to do so indirectly. It is an example of a doctrinal sermon from a Hispanic perspective.*

As I have often recommended that preachers do, once again I have chosen for today a text I would rather not have chosen.

> There were some present at that very time who told him of the Galileans whose blood Pilate had mingled with their sacrifices. And he answered them, "Do you think that these Galileans were worse sinners than all the other Galileans, because they suffered thus? I tell you, No; but unless you repent you will all likewise perish. Or those eighteen upon whom the tower in Siloam fell and killed them, do you think that

they were worse offenders than all the others who dwelt in Jerusalem? I tell you, No; but unless you repent you will all likewise perish." And he told them this parable: "A man had a fig tree planted in his vineyard; and he came seeking fruit on it and found none. And he said to the vinedresser, 'Lo, these three years I have come seeking fruit on this fig tree, and I find none. Cut it down; why should it use up the ground?' And he answered him, ' Let it alone, sir, this year also, till I dig about it and put on manure. And if it bears fruit next year, well and good; but if not, you can cut it down.' " (Luke 13:1-9 RSV)

This is a text most of us avoid, because it raises a number of thorny questions, particularly the age-old question of why human tragedies occur. When tragedy strikes, the first question we ask is, why? Why did my child have to die? What evil had he done? Was it perhaps for some evil I did? Why does famine strike in Africa? Is it perhaps because of some particular sinfulness of the Africans or their leaders? Why does Andrew hit Florida and not Georgia? Why did those people die in the accident in Pittsburgh, and not others? These are all questions that it is quite natural to ask and quite impossible to answer. And that is one of the reasons that we tend to stay away from this passage in the Gospel of Luke.

The other reason is that the passage does not answer those questions. As pastors, we have often found ourselves having to deal with this sort of question and wishing we had a ready-made answer, one that would immediately console the bereaved, enlighten the perplexed, and reassure the doubting. But Jesus does not give us, as we would like, a ready-made answer that we could give—like a doctor prescribes a pill to a patient—to the mother whose teen-age son has just died in an automobile accident. Rather, all that he does is to tell us that a certain answer is wrong, and then he moves on to tell us that such tragedies, unexplainable and mysterious though they may be, do call survivors to greater obedience.

Let us look more closely at the text. Jesus is on his way to Jerusalem, and he has been speaking about what it means to be a faithful people. In that context, someone comes and tells him of a gruesome crime that Pilate has perpetrated. He has mingled the blood of a number of Galileans with their sacrifices. In other words, he has killed them just as they were offering their sacrifices to God. The details of what had taken place are not altogether clear. But several things are clear.

The first is that this terrible crime took place in the temple in Jerusalem, for this was the place where the Galileans would have come to offer sacrifices to God.

The second is that, precisely because it had taken place in the temple, it was a most horrible crime. It was not only murder, but also sacrilege. One may well surmise that many Jews were reminded of the event, several decades earlier, when Pompey rode his horse into the holy of holies. Or that other time, many years earlier, when the temple was destroyed and the people led into captivity. We certainly are reminded of the murder of Becket before the high altar in the cathedral of Canterbury, or more recently, of the murder of Archbishop Oscar Romero under similar circumstances in a church in El Salvador.

Third, what becomes clear when we read the entirety of the Gospel is that there was a great deal of animosity on the part of some of the Jewish leaders in Jerusalem toward all Galileans. Indeed, many Jews viewed Galileans as second-class Jews, as standing somewhere between the true Jews and the heathenish Gentiles.

For all these reasons, those who are telling Jesus of Pilate's crime are raising several questions in one. They are raising first of all the question of the reason for such seemingly meaningless suffering. Second, they are raising the question of whether good Jews should not be incensed at Pilate and all the Romans. In other words, as in so many other places in the Gospel narrative, they are trying to place Jesus in the difficult position of having to appear either unpatriotic or subversive. If he condemns Pilate's act, he will be accused of inciting rebellion against the Romans. If he plays down its importance, his listeners will be outraged at his religious and human insensitivity. Finally, they are raising the question of the relations between Galileans and other Jews. In telling him of the horrible thing that has happened to these Galileans, they are raising the commonly held belief among Jews that Galileans were less faithful than other Jews. Perhaps this is the reason why Jesus responds: "Do you think that these Galileans were worse sinners than all the other Galileans?" (Luke 13:2 RSV). And then he sharpens the question by bringing it closer to home and referring to an incident in Jerusalem: "Those eighteen upon whom the tower of Siloam fell and killed them, do you think that they were worse offenders than all the others who dwelt in Jerusalem?" (Luke 13:4 RSV).

To me this entire text is particularly poignant because I have lost count of the number of times when, speaking to someone about hunger in various parts of the world, I have heard the response that these people are suffering from famine because of their sin. Or, when speaking of the suffering in our inner cities and our minority enclaves, I have also been told that such misery is the result of those people's sin. I do agree that famine and misery are the result of human sin, although very likely not the sin of those who are suffering and dying. Therefore, upon reading this text, I wonder if Jesus wouldn't have responded with something like: Do you believe that those Rwandan children who have starved to death were worse sinners than the rest of Africa, worse sinners than the ruthless and uncaring government under which they lived? Or the 126 who perished in the crash in Pittsburgh, do you think that they were worse offenders than all the others?

When we put the matter in such terms, it is clear that whatever we say about the suffering of those faraway must be consistent with what we are ready to say about the tragedies that strike closer to home, and even about our own suffering.

If we combine this with what the rest of Scripture says, it is clear that those who appear to be most blessed, or at least strongest, may cause some suffering. Hear for instance what the prophet Ezekiel has to say on the matter:

> Is it not enough for you to feed on the good pasture, that you must tread down with your feet the rest of your pasture; and to drink of clear water, that you must foul the rest with your feet? And must my sheep eat what you have trodden with your feet, and drink what you have fouled with your feet? (Ezek. 34:18-19 RSV)

Those words are from Ezekiel 34. I invite you to read the entire chapter, where you will find that often human suffering is the result of human sin, yes, but not necessarily the sin of those who suffer. You will also find, let me say in passing, that contrariwise to what we learned in Economics 101, it is not scarcity that causes greed, but rather greed that causes scarcity.

But, back to our Gospel text. There, Jesus carries the matter one step further, and shows that we are posing the question in the wrong way. The surprising thing is not that so many die. The even more surprising thing is that we still live. If it were a matter of sin, we would all be dead. Twice he says: "Unless you repent, you will all likewise perish" (13:3). And then he illustrates his meaning with a parable.

A man had a fig tree planted in his vineyard; and he came seeking fruit on it and found none. And he said to the vinedresser: "Lo, these three years I have come seeking fruit on this fig tree, and I find none" (13:7). Then a conversation ensues with the outcome that the owner of the vineyard agrees that for one more year the tree will be left to stand. It will even receive special care. But if at the end of that time it has not produced fruit, it shall be cut down.

What does the parable mean, in this context? It clearly means that those of us who survive, those Galileans who were not killed by Herod, or those Jews on whom the tower did not fall, or those of us who have not died from famine, or those whose airplane has not crashed, are living only by the grace of God, and that our continued life is for the purpose that we bear fruit.

It also means that even our apparent blessing and abundance is not necessarily something of which we should boast. The tree that has produced no fruit receives special attention and added fertilizer, not because it is so good, but rather because it is so poor.

In order to understand the poignancy of the parable, one has to remember what a vineyard looks like at the time when one would normally come looking for figs on a fig tree. The vineyard would have already yielded its grapes, and would already have been pruned. It would all have been cut down, and one would see nothing but dry and gnarled stumps. And, in the midst of this scene of apparent desolation, stands a verdant fig tree. It has never been pruned. It has been allowed to grow tall and green. Now, it will receive even further special treatment. The vinedresser will dig around it, and give it an exceptional dose of fertilizer. To a casual observer, the tree would appear to be specially blessed, and the vines cursed and forgotten, and one would think that the fig tree must be especially valuable if it is treated with such care. But the truth is exactly the opposite. The fig tree is receiving special care because it has yet to give the fruit it is meant to bear.

I said at the beginning that I do not particularly like this parable. And this is the final and true reason why I do not like it. I would like to think that the reason why I have a comfortable house, when so many are homeless, and a substantial income, when so many are poor, and all kinds of food to eat, when so many are hungry, and a relatively healthy body, when so many are ill, is that I have somehow been particularly faithful. I would like to think that the reason why I have already lived longer than the average person on this globe is because my life has been so productive.

This text, however, leads me to think otherwise. Could it be, could it just be, that the reason why I have been given all these advantages is that otherwise I would have great difficulty bearing fruit? Could it be that all these things of which I so pride myself are really just so much manure, piled on me because otherwise I'd be such a lousy fruit tree? It is a question I must ponder, a question that I invite you to ponder in the days ahead.

And what is a question for us as individuals and as families is also a question for us as a church and as individual congregations. We tend to admire the big church with the tall steeple, the large staff, and the professional choir. We tend to think that the fact that a church has many resources at its command is a sign that it has been faithful. But this parable raises the question—just the question—that it may really be otherwise. I have seen very poor churches, both in this country and overseas, churches with no social prestige, churches with no buildings, where one can breathe the Spirit of God, and where one can taste the fruits of mercy and justice. And I sometimes wonder—I just wonder—could it be that our own wealth of resources has been given to us in an effort to lead us to bear fruit, to share those resources, to share of ourselves, and that the reason we survive is, not our great budget, our nice music, our fine sermons, our beautiful buildings, our sophisticated theology, but this miraculous grace of the owner of the vineyard who has decided to give us one more chance?

Today, the owner of the vineyard invites us to the table to be fed. We come to the table of tables, to the foretaste of the heavenly banquet. We enjoy a privilege far above any other anyone might covet. It is time to rejoice! But, in the midst of our rejoicing, let us remember that, like a fruitless fig tree in the middle of God's vineyard, we are not being fed because of who we are, or what we have done, but rather because of that stubborn grace of God that insists on giving us one more chance. So be it! Amen.

CHAPTER NINE

CALLED TO CHEAT

(Luke 16:1-13)

Justo L. González

> *This sermon was delivered at Duke Divinity School's chapel in the fall of 2003. On that occasion, a number of Latino and Latina leaders gathered at Duke to discuss important issues related to the future of Hispanic ministries and theological education. In a way, this is a sermon about an administrator mainly addressed to church and seminary administrators. However, given that there were students also present at worship, the sermon tries to address people at many levels. Since this was a communion service, the sermon also interprets the text in light of the liturgical event.*

I have often told my students that it is important to preach now and then on a text we do not like. It keeps us honest. It keeps us struggling with Scripture. Therefore, in keeping with my own advice, I have chosen for today a text I would rather not have chosen: Luke 16:1-13, known as the parable of the unfaithful steward.

What makes this text difficult is that here Jesus takes a thief, a rascal, and uses him as an example for us. The parable of the sower speaks of a man who works for a living. The woman who put the leaven in the dough was also working. The parable of the talents speaks of three stewards who try to do their best. All of those are characters worthy of imitation, and their stories are often told in Christian art. But, can you imagine a stained glass window where a character with a shifty look tells another, "Where it says a hundred, put down eighty"?

Yet, in spite of all this, as I reflect on this parable, I realize that it makes much sense, for it accurately describes our situation.

The steward seems quite happy in his position when he receives the fateful news: his stewardship will be taken from him. What he would have liked to be permanent is not so.

We are in a similar condition. Sometimes we are so settled into life, managing and enjoying its goods, that we convince ourselves that we have a permanent post here. We forget the human condition is such that when we least expect it we may be fired. Thus, perhaps like the steward in the parable, we go about our business administering the things of life, and enjoying its goods as if our tenure would never end.

But the fact is that, like the steward in the parable, we have all been fired—at least, we have been given notice. The parable does not tell us how many days' notice the steward received. Nor do we know how many days are left until our firing is effective. But the fact remains that we are all on notice.

Perhaps this is the core of the parable. What does the steward do? One less wise would have followed one of two courses of action: first, he could say: "The master no longer wants me; his goods will no longer be mine to manage. Therefore, let him keep his riches. I want nothing to do with them." Or, second, he could say: "I have been fired, but I still have the power to manage these goods, I shall enjoy them while they last."

But this wise scoundrel does neither of these two things. What he says is: "These riches are not mine. The present order in which I am a manager will pass. Therefore, I shall now employ them, not as I would in the order that is passing, but rather in light of the future order."

We too have the same options as the steward. We know that we have been fired, that the present order is passing. What then shall we do with our present tenure? One possible answer is: "I'll enjoy all I can. Life is short and I am going to enjoy it." That is a common answer in our day, when people are frantically trying to make more money, to have more experiences, to enjoy more things. The second answer is also common among Christians: "Since all this is passing, I shall ignore and forget it. The material things of this life can lead me away from God. Therefore, I shall ignore them and pretend that they do not exist."

But the steward of the parable is wiser than that. What he says to himself is: "I need to use the owner's goods while I still have some control over them in order to make friends for myself that I can call upon when I need to in the future." So he changes the bills and indeed makes friends. When Jesus commends such actions, he says to us: "Make friends for yourself by means of dishonest wealth so that when it is gone, they may welcome you into the eternal homes."

But there is more, Jesus makes no bones about it. The riches of the present order are "unrighteous riches." It is not just that we shall die. It is also that the present order of injustice shall pass, that God's reign shall come; and yet, here and now, knowing that God's reign is at hand, I have much that I do not need nor deserve, while there are many who deserve just as much as I do, and yet do not have what they need.

What am I to do about it?

As in the case of the steward there are two common responses. One is to ignore the entire situation, to continue enjoying what I have as if this order of injustice would continue forever. The other is to reject what I have; to feel guilty about it to the point that I am paralyzed.

We are gathered here today in an impressive chapel, surrounded by art and beauty, while we know that millions live in horror and squalor. Many of us have just come from one of the best libraries of the world, while we know that millions cannot even read. We must not fool ourselves. We are the beneficiaries of unrighteous Mammon, we live as we do, not really because we have earned it, but because the world is an unjust place.

What are we to do? An easy solution is to hide from reality; to dig into our library and forget about the illiterate millions; to look at our stained glass and forget the real stains upon the world. Another possible outcome, perhaps more realistic, but equally fruitless, is to feel guilty and even to cherish our guilt as some perverted sort of virtue, and still do nothing about unrighteous Mammon.

But there is a third response: the wise response of the steward in the parable: I may use the unjust riches which I have to serve the order of justice that I know is coming. I may use what I learn in that library to bring knowledge and justice to those who lack it.

That is what we seek to do at this table today, when we still live in the midst of the old order, yet also celebrate the in-breaking of the new in the resurrection of Jesus. For the Lord Jesus, in the night in which he was betrayed, took bread—bread, a glaring symbol of the unjust disorder of the present order—bread which so many lack, while others have overmuch.

And he took wine, which he could have used to forget the pain and the injustice of his betrayal.

And of that bread and that wine he made his challenge to the present disorder and his promise of the coming order, when he shall drink wine with us in the kingdom. And so in his name we eat this bread and drink this wine. Bread, which is so unjustly distributed in this world, and which therefore, we can use to become paralyzed by guilt. Wine that could easily lead to callous overindulgence. But bread and wine, which by God's grace, become a sign, a promise and an instrument of God's coming order. So be it!

CHAPTER TEN

THE PAST OF OUR FUTURE

(Colossians 1:15-20)

Pablo A. Jiménez

In an earlier chapter of this book, Justo González affirms the strong connection between life and faith that is experienced by Hispanics. To borrow Carlos Mesters's phrase, Latinos and Latinas read "life in the Bible and the Bible in life."

This sermon establishes a clear correlation between the suffering experienced by the early Christian community and the suffering experienced by minority communities in the United States today. Although the sermon focuses on the Hispanic experience, it also makes reference to the experience of African Americans in our nation.

Another important trait is the way it addresses what González calls "a theology of eschatological subversion." The text affirms the ultimate victory of God over the forces of death and the transformation of the world it implies, thus sustaining the hope that Hispanics so desperately need in order to survive.

The Present

Puerto Rico, my homeland, is a rather small island in the Caribbean. It is thirty-five miles wide and one hundred miles long; nothing compared to Texas. Nevertheless, Puerto Rico has some endearing places, such as the township of Dorado.

Dorado, which roughly translated means "the golden one," is in the north-central section of the island. It stands about forty minutes away from San Juan, at the outskirts of the larger metro area. Dorado is known for its resorts, one of which boasts the "longest pool in the world" and world-class golf courses.

By the chain-link fence of one of those golf courses there is a slum. Actually, there are a number of them that were originally shantytowns. Little by little, the squatters bought their respective properties, transforming their wooden shacks into storm-resistant concrete houses.

My uncle Víctor and his family lived right in front of the chain-link fence that divided the world of the rich from the world of the poor. Víctor, like most of our family, belonged to the latter. He was the oldest of ten siblings. He was the first one who came in contact with the message of the gospel, joining a little Pentecostal church in his barrio.

But he also carried the family curse. Victor was an alcoholic who, in spite of his profound faith, relapsed time and again until his liver failed. Víctor died in his late forties.

The day of the burial our greatest concern was my grandmother, Doña Adela. She was in her sixties, frail and infirm. Her pint-size body suffered from emphysema, due to the many cigarettes she had smoked since her childhood. Her heart suffered from grief, given that Víctor was the second child she had lost in two years. My mom was the first.

Dorado is so close to the shoreline that its cemetery has sand instead of dirt. The little cascade of sand that fell from the heap to the grave told us we had to rush the burial. My grandmother almost fainted when the casket was lowered. Someone eased her to a chair. Then she began to clap her hands without much rhythm and to sing off key: *"Mi Dios y yo andamos siempre juntos."* "My God and I are always together," she sang.

- She sang because in her old age she had come to believe in the gospel of Jesus Christ.
- She sang because through her faith she had developed a memory that went back to Eve and Abel, Sarah and Isaac, Mary and Jesus.
- She sang because that glorious past promised a glorious future; a time and a place where God "will wipe every tear from their

eyes. Death will be no more; mourning and crying and pain will be no more, for the first things have passed away" (Rev. 21:4).

The Past

It is wise to sing a hymn in times of trial, particularly when that hymn reminds us of God's saving acts. That is the strategy followed by the book of Colossians in the reading for today. Clearly the churches in Colossae were in turmoil. On one hand, they were in a crisis of faith, due to the visit of missionaries who preached false doctrines. Apparently these missionaries interpreted the gospel through the eyes of Greek religion. They affirmed that Jesus was one among many spiritual beings (2:18). Although they affirmed that Jesus was at the top of the hierarchy, their interpretation of the gospel required the worship of the spiritual beings at the lower echelons of that "chain of command."

On the other hand, the churches in Colossae were in a social crisis. The Christian faith had recently been declared a "superstition" by Emperor Nero, triggering the persecution, imprisonment, and murder of thousands of believers in the Italian peninsula—a persecution that could readily extend and reach Colossae. Although things had calmed down, the Christian movement still refused to worship the Roman emperor. This fact placed the church at the fringes of society, leaving Christians open to accusations of treason, atheism, and hate of humanity.

All this explains the tone of urgency that characterizes the prayer that begins in verse 11: "May you be made strong with all the strength that comes from his glorious power, and may you be prepared to endure everything with patience, while joyfully giving thanks to the Father." The Colossian Christians needed endurance and patience. We can translate the word "endurance" also as "resistance" or "militant commitment." It is clear, then, that one of the aims of the letter to the Colossians is to call and equip the Christian community to resist the oppressive influence of the false missionaries and the Roman imperial ideology.

How can you equip a local congregation to resist evil? Well, how about a hymn!

Colossians proceeds to quote a hymn that was surely known to the congregation, a beautiful spiritual song that begins in verse 5:

He is the image of the invisible God, the firstborn of all creation; for in him all things in heaven and on earth were created, things visible and invisible, whether thrones or dominions or rulers or powers—all things have been created through him and for him. He himself is before all things, and in him all things hold together. He is the head of the body, the church; he is the beginning, the firstborn from the dead, so that he might come to have first place in everything. For in him all the fullness of God was pleased to dwell, and through him God was pleased to reconcile to himself all things, whether on earth or in heaven, by making peace through the blood of his cross. (1:15-20)

We do not know the original tune of this hymn. We do not even know its origin or its development. What we do know through the study of the Greek text is that it is indeed a hymn, even though in many translations it is not divided in stanzas.

It would be utterly impossible to discuss in depth the rich imagery of this text. Even to outline the hymn is a daunting task. However, its main idea is evident. This hymn exalts Christ as the true prince of the universe. Its memory goes to the times before creation, before time itself, finding Christ there. In beautiful poetic language, the hymn reminds us of our sacred past. A past where there is Christ:

- Christ, preexisting image of God
- Christ, architect and foreman of creation
- Christ, above all spiritual beings and powers
- Christ, head of a cosmic body
- Christ, the beginning
- Christ, firstborn from the dead
- Christ, above everything

This glorious past promises a glorious future.

- It promises the future reconciliation of everything in Christ.
- It promises a peace achieved "through the blood of his cross" (v. 20).
- It promises the ultimate triumph of life over the forces of death.

It was dangerous for the church to preach this message in the Roman Empire. This language is politically charged. The exaltation of Jesus as prince of the universe is in direct contradiction with the Roman use of the word "prince" as the proper title of the emperor. While the Empire hailed the emperor as the *princeps* or "first citizen" of the senate, the church hailed Christ as the "prince"

above creation,
above death,
above spiritual powers,
and above everything else.

The Present

It is difficult to picture such joy in the midst of suffering; such faith in the midst of death. To be blunt, it sounds kind of crazy. Can a little song make the difference?

I do not know. But history teaches us that in moments when all seemed lost, people of faith sang their way to hope. Among the many examples that we may recall, there is one that stands out in my mind. Slaves in the Southern part of the United States developed a rich hymnody. Some of their spiritual songs were also politically charged. One of those hymns is titled "O Freedom."

O freedom, O freedom, O freedom over me
And before I be a slave, I'll be buried in my grave
And go home to my Lord and be free.

To think that this hymn was actually composed by slaves is mind-boggling. Being in chains, they are vowing to die before being enchained.

How do you develop this crazy faith that thrusts a community of believers to hope against all hope? I do not know. Maybe it all begins when we remember God's creation, Christ's cross, and the early church's faith. Or maybe it all begins when a frail elderly lady, sitting by a fresh grave, claps her hands without much rhythm and sings off key: "My God and I are always together."

CHAPTER ELEVEN

THE PEARL

(Matthew 13:45-46)

Pablo A. Jiménez

Hispanics live between two worlds. On the one hand, we live in a Latino world where we speak mostly Spanish and relate mainly to other Hispanics. On the other hand, we live in a larger Anglo-European society where we speak mostly English and relate to people from different parts of the world. Sometimes those two worlds come together in a single congregation. Increasingly, Hispanic preachers address congregations where some members speak only one language, while others are bilingual.

The following sermon exemplifies a particular technique for bilingual preaching. In reality, there are two different sermons about the same topic, one in English and another in Spanish, preached alternatively. In this way, every hearer understands the sermon while bilingual hearers are not forced to hear the same sermon twice.

This particular sermon was preached at the installation service of Pastor Iluminado "Lumi" Castellano, at Emmanuel Christian Church in Mentor, Ohio.

Introduction

La parábola es uno de los géneros literarios más hermosos en las Sagradas Escrituras. Estas cortas historias son, a la misma vez, sencillas y profundas. Usan los asuntos más comunes—como la siembra, la pesca o la limpieza de una casa—para hablar del asunto más profundo que un ser humano pueda pensar: el reino de Dios. Podemos apreciar estas características en todas las parábolas que aparecen en las Sagradas Escrituras y, especialmente, en las parábolas de Jesús.

Jesus' parables are beautiful both for their content and for their form. However, interpreting the parables presents a major challenge for the church today. The fact is that the church has come to be too familiar with the parables. As we know, familiarity can breed contempt. In this case, the church has come to be so familiar with Jesus' parables that these enigmatic stories have lost their ability to surprise us. Indeed, they have lost their "scandal."

The Scandalous Parables

Cuando leemos los evangelios vemos que los líderes religiosos del tiempo de Jesús no recibieron sus parábolas con gozo. Por el contrario, la inmensa mayoría de los escribas, los fariseos, los saduceos, los herodianos, y los familiares de los sumos sacerdotes encontraron que estas parábolas eran escandalosas.

Jesus' parables have scandalous elements. They shocked their audience then, and they are meant to shock their audiences now. The aim of the parables is to shatter our way of understanding the world, inviting us to accept a new way of seeing and understanding reality.

El propósito de las parábolas es transformar nuestra manera de ver el mundo. Por eso, las parábolas intentan destruir nuestra vieja manera de comprender la realidad. Dios desea que veamos la vida a través de los ojos de la fe. Dios desea que interpretemos la vida a la luz de los valores de su reino. Dios desea que transformemos nuestra forma de pensar, hasta que lleguemos a tener la mente de Cristo.

In order to preach the parables properly, we need to read them and reread them until we find their scandalous elements. If your audience is too comfortable with the message of a given parable, you may not be preaching it correctly. We only interpret a parable properly when we find its scandal.

Pensémoslo bien. Si Jesús predicó sus parábolas con el propósito de cambiar radicalmente la forma como la gente de su época pensaba, queda claro que para predicar correctamente las parábolas es necesario recuperar sus elementos escandalosos. Si no comprendemos por qué el liderazgo del tiempo de Jesús pensaba que las parábolas eran ofensivas y escandalosas, no estamos listos para predicarlas.

Rereading the Parables

For all these reasons, I propose that we need to reread the parables, trying to find each one's "scandal." As an example, let us consider the parable of the lost sheep (Matt. 18:10-14). We all know the story, don't we? A shepherd loses one of the hundred sheep that composed his flock. As soon as he realizes it, he leaves the other ninety-nine secure in their pen while he goes and looks for the lost one. This parable teaches us about God's unconditional love for humanity, for God is like the shepherd who rescues us every time we stray. Right? Well, no, that interpretation is incorrect. The text never mentions a pen. The text never tells us that the ninety-nine sheep were secured. On the contrary, the text states that he left the ninety-nine "on the mountains" while looking for the other one. The other element that we must bear in mind is that most shepherds were not the owners of the sheep. Now, be honest with me, if you were caring for a hundred sheep and you lost only one, would you risk losing the other ninety-nine?

¿Por qué la gente del tiempo de Jesús encontró escandalosa la parábola del sembrador (Mateo 13:1-9)? La mayor parte de nosotros no la encontramos escandalosa. Repasemos, pues, la historia. Un sembrador echó semilla en cuatro tipos de terrenos distintos. El sembrador representa a Dios, la semilla al mensaje del evangelio y los terrenos a distintos tipos de personas. Cuando el mensaje del evangelio cae en un corazón receptivo, la semilla da el fruto adecuado. Esta es la interpretación correcta, ¿No? Pues fíjese bien que no, esta no es la interpretación correcta. La historia nos enseña que un terreno promedio en la Palestina antigua daba poco más de cuatro medidas de grano por cada medida de semilla. Es decir, si usted sembraba un kilo de semilla, podría esperar un promedio de 4.8 kilos de grano. En el valle del Sarón, dónde están los terrenos más fértiles de Israel, las cosechas podían llegar a dar entre seis a ocho medidas de grano por cada medida de semilla. En el caso de la parábola del sembrador, las cosechas dieron treinta por uno, sesenta por uno y hasta cien por uno. Es decir, lo que la parábola describe es sencillamente imposible.

The message of the parable of the lost sheep is not about unconditional love, but about risk. The loving shepherd is willing to risk the well-being of the ninety-nine sheep and, thus, his own well-being, for the lost sheep. Through this parable, God calls us to risk our all for the kingdom of God. Through this parable, God tells us about the divine willingness to risk it all in order to reach one lost person.

El mensaje de la parábola del sembrador es que el reino de Dios da frutos insospechados y hasta increíbles. Cuando el reino se encarna en un lugar, los resultados son sorprendentes, inesperados y hasta imposibles de creer.

The Pearl

Let us turn our attention to the parable of the pearl.

Sobre esta base, consideremos el contenido y el mensaje de la Parábola de la Perla de Gran Precio.

The parable of the pearl is simple enough. A merchant who specializes in trading pearls finds one that is very expensive. Then, he sells everything he has in order to buy it.

De primera intención, la Parábola parece ser muy sencilla. Un mercader que se dedicaba a comerciar perlas encuentra una muy valiosa. Entonces, vende todo lo que tiene y la compra. Todo esto parece lógico, hasta que ponderamos las consecuencias de la acción del mercader. Noten que este hombre vende todo lo que tiene con el propósito de comprar la perla, pero en ningún momento se dice que piensa revenderla. Al comprar la perla, este hombre ha tomado una opción transformadora y fundamental: ha abandonado el comercio de perlas. Ha decidido abandonar el "juego" de la compra y venta para poder quedarse con esta perla en particular. El mercader lo ha sacrificado todo por la perla valiosa.

We may miss the fact that the parable implies that the merchant is keeping the pearl. He is not selling this one. The pearl is so valuable and so beautiful that he intends to keep it, even if that means abandoning the trade. He is rich, owning such a stunning pearl. But he is also broke, because he has spent all he had, and he is keeping the pearl. As all others, this parable contains a teaching about the kingdom of God. The "scandal" of this parable is that we must be willing to abandon everything for sake of the kingdom. Like the merchant, God calls us to sacrifice everything for the "pearl's" sake.

Sí, Dios nos llama a sacrificarlo todo por la perla. Dios nos llama a abandonar todas aquellas cosas que consideramos preciosas o hermosas con tal de alcanzar el reino. Dios nos llama a abandonar nación, trabajo y todas aquellas cosas que puedan darnos seguridad material con tal de alcanzar su reino.

Conclusion

En esta hora estamos reunidos con el propósito de instalar al hermano Iluminado Castellano como pastor de la Iglesia Emmanuel en Mentor, Ohio.

We are gathered today with the special purpose of installing brother Iluminado Castellano as pastor of Emmanuel Christian Church in Mentor, Ohio. There are plenty of good things to be said about Lumi. We can spend a good chunk of time extolling his many virtues, like his meekness, his loving heart, and his unending cheerfulness.

En esta mañana he decidido resaltar sólo un elemento que caracteriza a Iluminado. Aparte de ser un buen esposo, un padre dedicado y un pastor amoroso, Lumi es del dueño de una hermosa perla, una perla de gran precio. Tardó mucho en comprarla, pues tuvo que ahorrar por años para poder pagar su precio. Pero ahora, habiendo sacrificado todo por la perla, no la venderá jamás.

Every time I read the parable of the pearl, I think about those who have sacrificed everything for the gospel of Jesus Christ. Lumi is one of those persons. It is with great joy, that I introduce you to Pastor Iluminado Castellano, who is the proud owner of a pearl of great price: A pearl for which he has sacrificed everything; a pearl that he will never trade.

CHAPTER TWELVE

COME TO THE JORDAN MOMENTS

(Luke 3:21-22)

Joel N. Martínez

Bishop Joel N. Martínez, a Mexican American United Methodist minister, who was born and raised in Seguin, Texas, has extensive pastoral experience. He is the resident bishop of the San Antonio Area, and chairs the General Board of Global Ministries of The United Methodist Church.

This sermon was originally preached at a gathering of the Nebraska Annual Conference of Learning, which is the pastors' annual school. Its main purpose is to call listeners to renew their baptismal vows, as they offer themselves in ministry, particularly to the poor. The sermon also makes reference to Methodist history, particularly to an episode of John Wesley's life. Once again, notice how the Hispanic preacher blends personal history and biblical reflection.

This coming Sunday is Baptism of the Lord Sunday in the Christian calendar. The celebration of Jesus' baptism is a strong tradition in the Eastern Church, but much neglected in the Western church. Indeed, in the Eastern Church this is the season of the Epiphanies—plural—of Jesus. These include the birth, the baptism, and the first miracle at Cana.

Having just celebrated the season of the extraordinary star and having been illumined by the greater brightness shining in the manger, I would invite us to journey to the banks of Jordan. The Gospel of Luke records it was here, in responding to the preaching of John, that another of the epiphanies happened. As the waters washed over Jesus, so did a clearer sense of his identity, his calling, and his future take hold of his mind and heart. In his identification with others coming to John, whom Jesus later called the greatest of the prophets, Jesus was stepping into the ancient stream of righteousness history which flowed clear and fresh again through the preaching of the Baptizer. When Jesus stepped into the waters, he stepped into a particular struggle; he joined with a particular company, and assumed a particular mission.

Thomas Moore, in his book *Care of the Soul*, describes what baptism symbolizes for any person struggling with decisions about life's purpose. He comments on a painting by Píero della Francesca showing Jesus standing in the river about to be baptized. Behind Jesus another man waits his turn. It is, writes Moore, "an image of the willingness to step courageously into the river of existence, instead of finding ways to remain safe, dry, and unaffected."[1]

In Luke's telling of Jesus' baptism, there is the confirming voice, "You are my son ... with you I am well pleased" (Luke 3:22). There is also the descent of the dove, a sign of the Spirit's empowering presence. In Luke's theology, the coming of the Spirit is God's initiative to prepare Jesus and the church to move into mission (Acts 1:8, 3:1-4). Inward confirmation and outward sign of the call, personal awareness and public manifestation, are joined in the experience.

But Jesus was not spared the ambiguity of struggling with the servant identity he embraced. Stepping into Jordan's baptismal waters, Jesus was no longer "safe, dry, and unaffected." In the waters of baptism we are not freed from inner struggle; we are drawn deeper into it.

For Jesus, the path from Jordan is through the desert where temptation abounds. Desert, for Jesus and for us, is less a place than a recurring experience. Some of today's temptations seem quite clear: choosing to remain safely on the riverbank of calculating middle-class charity or stepping into the turbulent waters of justice ministry? Will we limit ourselves to the dry, comfortable ground of an ethnically homogeneous parish, or risk the uncertainties and possibilities of our increasingly diverse community? Do we remain within the reach and touch of the hungry and dispossessed, or build our new church facilities at ever-safer distances from them?

You and I were baptized into these struggles. If we are living out our baptism, these tensions are unavoidable.

Baptized into Community

Our baptism was in community and into community. The whole congregation assumed responsibility for our nurture; but we assumed that community's heritage, did we not?

I am reminded of my own baptism at La Trinidad United Methodist Church, in Seguin, Texas. This was a Mexican American community of believers in the Wesleyan tradition who embraced me and nurtured me into the faith. A people of deep faith, these sharecroppers, farm workers, domestics, and washerwomen accompanied me through the early steps of my faith journey.

Now, baptism into the Wesleyan heritage means a distinct call to learn and practice the faith as both personal and social holiness. If I read Wesley's thought and appreciate his practice correctly, we divide these at our peril.

To cite one example: the preaching at Bristol. George Whitefield and others challenged Wesley to preach to the multitudes of miners in that local coal-mining region. The proper cleric who was used to university chapel and cathedral pulpit was simply aghast at doing open air preaching; and this among miners, working-class poor, marginal people. It was for Wesley, a "Come to the Jordan moment." At Bristol he stepped into a stream where he found rebirth as a preacher and began his long career as an unconventional pastor among the poor and dispossessed. The deepening spiritual experience at Aldersgate empowered Wesley to widen his understanding of parish and to build faith communities beyond the boundaries of social class.

This community is the company with whom I have walked since my baptism. You too.

The particular community that baptized me spoke my name in Spanish. That is why it is Joel beginning with the "H" sound! On a long-ago day in 1966 this community reminded me in a special way about the meaning of my baptism.

In the summer of 1966, a group of *campesinos*, farm workers, undertook a 400-mile march from the lower Rio Grande Valley in South Texas to the state capitol at Austin. Their cause was justice and their demands modest ones: a minimum hourly wage of $1.25 and humane working conditions. These Mexican American workers captured the imagination of the Hispanic community of the state, as well as many sympathetic supporters, especially among the laboring poor and the churches.

I joined the march near Kennedy, Texas, about halfway to Austin. On the day I joined, I happened to be walking alongside the co-leaders of the march: Father Antonio Gonzales and the Reverend James Novarro, a Southern Baptist preacher. Shortly after I joined them, Gonzales and Novarro were called away by a television crew that pulled alongside. Novarro turned to me and said, "Here, carry these," and they walked off. What he handed me were the symbols of the march: a small U.S. flag and a Mexican flag, a crucifix, and a picture of the Virgin of Guadalupe, the Patron Saint of Mexico. This was a come to the Jordan moment for me. Because in that moment, as a middle-class, educated, Protestant steeped into a stream of history that served to confirm the meaning of my own baptism, I was drawn there by the prophetic work of "tenders of sycamore trees" that is, farm workers who raised their voices and linked their bodies to challenge greed and exploitation in the prophetic tradition of Amos.

On that July afternoon in 1966 near Kennedy, Texas, I stepped into the ancestral stream of my people's struggle for justice. As a Hispanic Protestant, suddenly bearing the people's symbols of cross, flag, and popular religion, I could not remain "dry, safe, and unaffected." I was, in a still inexplicable way, inwardly assured that I was one of the people. My sharecropper grandfathers and mothers would surely want me here with these marchers. I was never more my ancestors' child than at that moment. My calling to bear witness to Christ was renewed. There was no voice breaking from above! It was the voices and the acceptance of the poor, which were the signs of the Spirit's presence.

All of us are baptized into community. Reflect today on the communal heritage that embraces you and challenges you to serve God's mission.

Baptized into Mission

Jesus' baptism is followed by the desert experience. His initial public ministry in his hometown synagogue follows this. Jesus goes home to preach. He preaches his inaugural sermon. Quoting Isaiah's vision of a servant who will speak good news to the poor, announce freedom for captives, help the blind see again, and lift the oppressor's yoke, he declares this has come true at last. "Today this scripture has been fulfilled" (Luke 4:21). But there was more! You see, what got Jesus in trouble was not the choice of Scripture, but his choice of illustrations! You recall that he cited the examples of the starving widow at Zarephath and the Syrian leper, Naaman, as believers worthy of emulation by the skeptical crowd of listeners. Jesus' first sermon brings the enemy, the persons of no account, into the center of God's saving history. God's people are drawn from beyond the children of Abraham!

This would be a pattern by the writer of Luke-Acts. Another dramatic example is found in Acts 10. At a decisive moment for the mission of the early church, God uses a man from the wrong demographics, from the wrong level on the social pyramid, and certainly from the wrong end of the political spectrum to save Peter and the church from a possible implosion into obscurity and irrelevance. The Roman centurion takes Peter and the church toward strange people where the ever-inclusive God has already been! (Acts 10: 1-15).

The biblical witness according to Luke is that Jesus turned to the little ones as he wrestled with the question of God's mission. The way from Jordan for him led to embracing widows and Syrians, Roman centurions, and other Gentiles as the citizens of the new community of God's reign. Was it not by miners and other poor that Wesley was set free from overbearing tradition and came to think more mightily of God?

On a hot, summer day, I also experienced freedom and the blessing of renewed calling through courageous farm workers who refused to remain "safe, dry, and unaffected."

Remember Your Baptism

In the ritual of baptismal vows, the pastor is to declare to the congregation: "Remember who you are, remember your baptism." David remembered who he was during a volunteer in mission work camp in Havana in 1989. MARCHA, the Hispanic caucus of The United Methodist Church, organized the experience. While working on a government-sponsored project to build a bakery, David became friends with a young man whose wife had just given birth to their first child. The young father asked David to baptize the baby at the hospital even though it was not legal to do so. Religious rites were permitted only within church buildings in Cuba. David came to me for consultation since I was coordinator of our team. We agreed that his calling as an ordained minister left him no choice but to baptize the child. He did.

The renewal of our baptismal vows happens when we follow Christ from the Jordan into ministry with the little ones. This is the direction of Christ's mission and the calling to Christ's church.

Note

1. Thomas Moore, *Care of the Soul* (New York: Harper Collins, 1992), p. 244.

CHAPTER THIRTEEN

THE SPIRITUALITY OF THE CROSS

(Matthew 10:5a, 34-42)

Yolanda Pupo-Ortiz

Yolanda Pupo-Ortiz is an elder member of the Baltimore-Washington Conference of The United Methodist Church. She received her theological education at the Seminario Evangélico in Cuba and obtained a Master in Library Science at Emory University. She has served as a pastor and is a frequent writer for El libro de Programa de Mujeres Metodistas and for Lecciones Cristianas. She has taught at several Schools of Missions and at the Academy for Spiritual Formation. She also teaches at the Garrett-Evangelical Theological Seminary Course of Studies.

This sermon was preached at the Women and the Word event held at Boston University on March 14, 1996. The sermon exemplifies Hispanic interest in spirituality. It also highlights how Latinos and Latinas make theological reinterpretations of their own personal history, offering testimonios *(autobiographical sermons).*

Introduction: Our Reality

A friend of mine encountered Jesus and received the call to the ministry at the same time. The only son of an anarchist father (his mother had died when he was only three), he had been raised with all kinds of expectations to follow in his father's steps. He was already in the second year of his university studies when a friend invited him to church, a small Methodist church in Cuba. It was in that church that unexpectedly one day he felt the "strange warm heart" that so many people describe in their conversion experience, among them our own John Wesley, and on the same day he felt the call to leave everything else to go into the ministry. He could not believe it! After the first moment he tried to resist the call. After all, he told himself, he could be a good Christian in the profession he had chosen. But it was too strong and he had to succumb to it. When I met him, he was already in seminary. With tears in his eyes he was telling his story to the class. To become a Christian and his call to the ministry had cost him his family. They had disowned him. This was the second year after that experience and they were still apart.

Have you had any experiences like that? I am sure you have. Remember those moments of decision when you had to decide to compromise or to stand by your principles; those times when to follow the dictates of your faith brought you apart from friends and even close family members; and those moments when you were the only one not laughing at a joke. Those moments when you had to speak up even if that meant breaking the harmony of the group. Those times when you had no other choice but to take sides with those who were oppressed, even if the ones on the other side were your own pastor, your wife, husband, parents, beloved teacher, or friend. Think about it. I want to give you a moment to recall such a difficult and challenging moment in your life. (Give here a few minutes for people to reflect and recall their own experiences.)

I wish we had time to share our stories, because I am sure you have brought to life some of yours. We all have stories that have left us marked. We all have stories to tell. Although the Bible and the history before us have given us many heroes and heroines of faith, we do not have to go far into history to encounter some of them, to witness courage and discipleship. There are many contemporary heroes and heroines, and you are among them.

The Scripture: Judged by God

We do not have time to share our stories now, but what I want all of us to do with the experiences that we have recalled is to take them with us as we go back to the Scripture passage we read. Under the light of our experiences, the passage all of a sudden does not sound so threatening. This is indeed a passage difficult to understand, especially if we take it out of context. Jesus' words were hard to hear. Was he really saying he had come to set a man against his father, a daughter against her mother? How could Jesus say such a thing? I remember an older lady in my neighborhood whose message to the children always was: "You have to obey and be respectful to your parents. That is one of Jesus' commandments and should be the number one commandment for you." We all agree that indeed to love and respect one's parents is an important commandment. Then what? Was Jesus contradicting himself? No, of course not. He loved his mother and we all know that being a Christian makes us better sons, daughters, husbands, wives, and so on. Let us read carefully the passage again. These hard words come at a very important moment. Jesus was sending the disciples out for ministry and he was giving them instructions. Using our words today, he was training them for the task. He was anticipating for them all the things that they would encounter. Jesus was enabling them to understand the true meaning of discipleship.

The Meaning of Being Jesus' Disciple

What is the meaning of being Jesus' disciple? In our own words:

- To be Jesus' disciples means our faith is first, and everything we do is guided by it.
- To be a disciple means to speak the truth even if that creates conflict.
- To be a disciple means to seek not one's life, but Life for all.
- To be a disciple means to love and to give ourselves to others so that *together* we may find shalom.
- To be a disciple means to identify with the pain and the hurts of the world, not only of those faraway from us, but also of those who are very near, those with whom we speak every day, those we encounter in the streets of our cities who are poor, homeless, and sick, those who are totally excluded from society.
- To be a disciple means to take the cross because it is in the cross that we are able to be disciples. We cannot be disciples without taking the cross. There is no growth without the

suffering of the cross in the same manner that there is no resurrection without the suffering of death.

The Spirituality of the Cross: Action

In my home church, a Quaker church, we did not have a cross. They
did not believe external symbols were necessary for your inner spiritual
growth. However, the cross was central to their faith and their life in the
midst of our community. They taught me, early and well, the spirituality
of the cross. They taught me that only in giving yourself totally, from the
inside (which is sometimes the most difficult part to surrender), can you
realize all your potential. Spiritual growth was very important in my little church, and I learned early that spiritual growth is not an individual
thing. Yes, you have to develop your spiritual life; you have to learn to
pray; you have to relate to God personally; but that is not all. You are part
of a community, you have responsibilities for others and others have
them for you. That was taught to us at church and at school. My sixth-
grade teacher was a creative and fun teacher. One day when we returned
from chapel we found that our teacher had gone ahead of us and was
already at his desk smiling in a mischievous way. On the floor there were
several books that apparently somebody had dropped. One by one we
entered the room and sat in our chairs, except one. One boy bent down,
put the books aside, and then sat down. The teacher then asked him: "Do
you mean to tell me that you were the only one at chapel?" The boy
looked at the teacher as surprised by his comments as we all were. "What
do you mean, teacher?" he asked. "What do you do in chapel?" continued our teacher. "Singing, praying, listening to the sermon—no? I think
this boy was the only one who did that because he is the only one who
took the time to put the books aside so that others would not fall."

Spiritual growth is reaching out to others, is being part of a community—not only the community of the church (where people think alike),
but the God-given community of all people. Spiritual growth is obtained
through self-giving, because real self-giving leads us to see others in a different light, leads us to open ourselves to the gifts of others. The maxi-
mum expression of that kind of self-giving is the cross. Henry Nouwen
tells us of his experiences as a pastor of a mentally handicapped community. He left seminary teaching in order to go and help them. He was feeling

pretty good about himself. For him that was a sacrifice. Yet, he found that in spite of his good intentions he was not communicating and reaching them, until the day when he began to open himself to be taught and led by them. He received much growth from those he had thought little ones.

The Road of the Cross: *Las procesiones de la cruz*

I am sure that Jesus made the disciples uncomfortable when he mentioned the cross. Sometimes we too are uncomfortable, not only because we do not like to suffer, or do not understand what Jesus was really saying, but also because the cross has been misinterpreted for too long. For too long people thought that the road of the cross was to gain our own salvation. The cross of Jesus is not for us to gain forgiveness or sanctification. I remember that when I was younger, to refer to a woman saying that she was *una mártir* was supposed to be a compliment. That usually meant that this woman did not think about herself at all; that she always put everybody else before her no matter what; that she sacrificed and smiled when people said how good she was. No, Jesus is not asking us to be that kind of martyr. Jesus is not asking us to submit ourselves to suffering for the purpose of our "own sanctification" or for the purpose of gaining the reign of God after we die. Women and people of color know well how this kind of thought has wounded their lives. Jesus' cross and his invitation to take the cross are broader and deeper than that.

It is difficult for us to get the true meaning of Jesus' invitation because we do not linger long enough on the cross. We try to jump over the cross quickly. Even during Holy Week, not many people come to church; not just Monday, Tuesday, and Wednesday, but not even Maundy Thursday and Good Friday. Easter Sunday is the big day and that is the goal of all preparations. After Easter, we do not sing again the hymns that belong to Good Friday, we do not want to remember the pain that the cross represents. The Spanish painters impressed me because they emphasized the suffering of Christ on the cross much more than Easter. In Cuba, Holy Week was indeed holy time. An important event during that week, especially for Roman Catholics, but in reality for the entire community, was *la procesión*. *La procesión* began at church. Church was the starting point, and then they would go all around town. There was no dialogue. The background was music, sad music. People in and joining the procession lived again the pain and humiliation of Christ. The women were weeping, the men wore black, and the children were very quiet. High above the procession was the Virgin Mary, full of tears, surrounded by the disciples. Judas and the people who wanted Jesus dead were in it. Then in the middle of the procession was Jesus painfully carrying the cross. You could see and experience the intensity of the pain. When I was a girl I had mixed feelings about the processions. I wanted to be there but at the same time I did not like them very much because they were too tragic. I did not like to see so much suffering. But I stayed there. I was captured by the procession and the tears became my tears; the pain became my pain. The procession went on filling the town with the cross of Jesus. Later on I discovered the real meaning of the *procesiones*; how important they were. I have understood that as long as we are on this earth, where the kingdom of God is already working but not totally fulfilled, we need the road of the cross. The road of the cross is identifying with the hurt of prejudice and discrimination, poverty and violence, drug abuse and unemployment, sexual harassment and child abuse. The road of the cross is becoming a poor with the poor, a marginal person with the marginal one, not by denying what we are, our education, resources, nationalities, and so on, but by taking up their cause and working with them for healing, for shalom.

I now know that those processions were in reality *procesiones de vida*, because the road of the cross is the road of life. As the procession went around town touching lives with the pain of the cross, it was also encircling the community with the abundant life that can be only found in the self-giving love and victory over death of the cross. We are called to become part of that procession of life—the church as the body of Christ—living in the world, identifying with the world, in a movement of solidarity that touches everyone with a new faith, and a new hope.

The call to take the cross is the call to choose life, and life in abundance. The call to take the cross is the call to shalom.

CHAPTER FOURTEEN

SACRIIFICE ON MOUNT MORIAH

(Genesis 21:1-2)

Roberto A. Rivera

Roberto A. Rivera is a retired Church of God (Cleveland) minister, who has served as a local pastor, district supervisor, director of Editorial Evangélica, president of the Colegio Bíblico Pentecostal in Puerto Rico and president of the Church of God seminary in Manila, Philippines. After earning a Ph.D. in education, his career was cut short by a massive heart attack that he miraculously survived. In spite of his health issues, he is active preaching, teaching, lecturing, and writing.

This expository sermon exemplifies Hispanics' high view of the authority of Scripture. Readers will notice how the preacher easily links the Hebrew Scriptures with New Testament teachings. The Bible is thus seen as the authoritative and transforming word of God.

Introduction

The novel *A Mysterious Stranger*, by the American author Mark Twain, portrays the parable of a God who acts haphazardly, destroying creatures for sport. He shows no compassion for humans. Instead, he would kill them without second thoughts, the way one would kill a worthless bug.

Unfortunately, some Christians perceive the God of the Bible not unlike the mysterious stranger of Twain's tale. A case in point is the way we sometimes interpret the incident between the Lord and Abraham regarding the sacrifice of Isaac.

A Stumbling Block

God's order to Abraham, to offer his son Isaac as a human sacrifice, posits a theological stumbling block for many believers. The apparent easiness with which the patriarch set out to comply with the heavenly instructions is, to say the least, astounding. It looks as if the Lord of the covenant were just another whimsical, bloodthirsty Canaanite deity, who had innocent children murdered in order to fulfill some cruel requirements.

The common explanation is that this was only a test of Abraham's obedience. This sounds unconvincingly shallow. On one hand, why submit a defenseless lad to such an inhuman torture in order to test his dad? On the other, had Abraham not proved his unswerving faith when he heeded the call to forsake his fatherland and sojourn into an unknown, hostile territory? This new nightmare requires a more intense purpose than a simple spiritual shibboleth.

Visible Sign of Faith

The key to the theological dilemma rests on an assessment of the place Isaac occupied in his father's heart. For Abraham, Isaac was more than the child of his old age; he was his whole reason for living. Since the very moment he accepted the first call in the Chaldean country, Abraham's life was consecrated to a goal greater than himself; that of becoming the father of a nation and the blessing of all families on earth (Gen. 12:2, 3; 17:2-8).

Isaac was the only link connecting the aging patriarch to his goal. To sacrifice him, as God demanded, was to relinquish any purpose for his past or his future, to eliminate the only visible sign of his faith. The trial entailed, therefore, the profoundest of spiritual experiences, and not merely a test of blind obedience. Picture, if you will, the biblical process of God's relationship to humans. God makes a promise. The promise may be either conditional or unconditional, but it ultimately depends on

God's faithfulness to the divine word. Man and woman respond in dependence on God's promise and trust in God's final purpose. Abraham's sacrifice probed the very essence of this process, to the extent that it jeopardized God's ability to fulfill the promise.

Evidence of Things Not Seen

It is one thing to walk confidently to a promised land, when you know it is somewhere beyond the horizon. It is altogether different to keep on trusting in the promise when everything is irreversibly lost, when the object of one's faith is no longer visible. As a matter of fact, before the birth of Isaac, Abraham had designed a scheme to help God with the missing heir. But the Lord had insisted adamantly that Isaac was the sign of the promise. In a seemingly cruel act of injustice, God had forced the aching father to get rid of Ishmael, the backup heir as it were. Now God wanted the boy, "your only son Isaac, whom you love," dead. This God of Abraham is unpredictable!

Or is God really so? Is faith not precisely "being sure of what we hope for and certain of what we do not see" (Heb. 11:1 NIV)? In order to fulfill the divine purpose, God required faith. And that in turn demanded the death of the one thing in the field of vision of the father of faith. It made no difference whether that thing was a piece of land, a herd of cattle, or even an heir-apparent.

The sacrifice on Mount Moriah was not a practical joke, but a frightful reality. It required believing in hope against all hope. So, "without weakening in his faith, he faced the fact that his body was as good as dead—since he was about a hundred years old—and that Sarah's womb was also dead. Yet he did not waver through unbelief regarding the promise of God, but was strengthened in his faith, and gave glory to God, being fully persuaded that God had power to do what he had promised" (Rom. 4:19-21 NIV).

Faith Is Not Cheap

Snoopy, the dog character from the *Peanuts* cartoon gang, complains, "When something bad is going to happen to you, there shouldn't be a night before." He had been accused of refusing to chase rabbits, and he had to appear before the head beagle's grand jury. He spends a sleepless night, tossing and turning, with nightmares about the worst possible outcomes. As it turned out, "the night before" was much more traumatic that the trial itself. But poor old Snoopy had no way of foretelling that!

It was the same with Abraham. We miss the point when we assume that the pain of Isaac's death did not happen. Actually, without the exquisitely painful sacrifice, that throughout three endless days was offered within Abraham's very entrails, all other sacrifices would have been "a resounding gong or a clanging cymbal." Every single drop of the son's blood was shed in the altar of the patriarch's feelings, hopes, dreams, and expectations.

It is easy for the modern mind to lose the perspective of the drama and conclude that Abraham foresaw the outcome of the trial. That would have made matters easier, but unfortunately, it was not so. (Or perhaps it was better this way, for otherwise; the whole event would be no more than a divine mockery.) At any rate, the only reason why Isaac did not perish literally on Moriah was because he actually died where he did have to die, namely, in his father's heart, in order to be resurrected into God's ultimate design. The substitute ram that took Isaac's place in the altar of stone was no substitute for the agony on the road to Moriah.

> By faith Abraham, when God tested him, offered Isaac as a sacrifice. He who had received the promises was about to sacrifice his one and only son, even though God had said to him, "It is through Isaac that your offspring will be reckoned." Abraham reasoned that God could raise the dead, and figuratively speaking, he did receive Isaac back from the dead. (Heb. 11:17-19 NIV)

Actually, the anticipated death of his son was not the only price of the patriarch's faithful obedience. Few readers realize that after the ordeal Abraham did not dare return to the boy's mother. Just imagine the elderly Sarah's reaction when she heard what that crazy fool had tried to do to her only son. Talk to her about heavenly visions and human holocausts! Abraham knew better than to reason with a distressed mother's rage. So, instead of going back home in Kiriath Arba, "Abraham returned to his servants, and they set off together for Beersheba. And Abraham stayed in Beersheba" (Gen. 22:19 NIV). Apparently, estrangement prevailed where once there was love and affection. It is safe to assume that Sarah never forgave him, for he did not go back to Kiriath Arba except for her funeral several years later. Faith is not cheap.

Conclusion

There can be no fullness of life without resurrection, but there can be no resurrection without a Calvary. How often do we struggle in vain, searching for a detour, a byroad, an alternate course to be risen with Christ, without having first died with Christ! It is a futile search. The only way to the garden of the empty tomb crosses over the hill of the skull. And there will be no substitute ram on top of Moriah until the sacrificial blood is shed in the altar of our hearts, for "without the shedding of blood there is no forgiveness" (Heb. 9:22 NIV).

The Lord of the Covenant is not Twain's mysterious stranger. He is "a man of sorrows, and familiar with suffering" (Isa. 53:3 NIV). For our own good, God cannot allow idols in our spiritual field of vision, even if it takes a living holocaust to get rid of them. God knows how idols contaminate our faith and cause us to miss the mark of abundant life for us. God knows that the predicate "your only... whom we love" can only have one Subject.

Perhaps, God is asking us today to take the lonesome road to Moriah. God could well be demanding that we offer in holocaust some of the choicest blessings God has given us. Our God is greater than any gifts, greater than all of God's gifts for that matter. So, when one of God's gifts becomes a visible object of faith, God may demand its demise. Whatever person, thing, possession, accomplishment, attitude, either physical or spiritual, might be enthroned in our holy of holies, the exclusive and inalienable abode of the Divinity, has to be sacrificed.

Who, or what, could be the Isaac of my life? Will I force him to be a needless victim in the holocaust God is demanding from me in my Mount Moriah? Must the knife fall before I understand the essence of the divine motif of love?

Hispanic Preaching: A Comprehensive Bibliography

Articles and Essays

Arrastía, Cecilio. "Predicadores y predicadores." *Pastoralia* 4:9 (Diciembre 1982), pp. 40-43.

———. "Teología para predicadores." *Pastoralia* 4:9 (Diciembre 1982), pp. 47-59.

———. "La iglesia: Comunidad hermenéutica." *Pastoralia* 4:9 (Diciembre 1982), pp. 67-73.

Bonilla, Plutarco. "Cecilio Arrastía: El hombre, el escritor y el predicador." *Pastoralia* 4:9 (Diciembre 1982), pp. 6-35.

Cortés, Benjamín. "Kerigma, mística, proposiciones." *Xilotl* 18:9 (Diciembre 1996), pp. 51-58.

Costas, Orlando E. s.v. "Predicación evangélica en América Latina" in *Diccionario de Historia de la Iglesia*. Edited by Wilton M. Nelson. (Miami: Editorial Caribe, 1989).

Demetrio, Yolanda; Blanca Cortés; Violeta y Rocha. "Haciendo la predicación con sentido de mujer: Metodologías, temas y desafíos de la predicación." *Xilotl* 18:9 (Diciembre 1996), pp. 59-82.

Figueroa, Juan. "El valor del pensamiento en la predicación cristiana." *El Educador Cristiano*, Tercera época (Febrero 1990), pp. 16-18.

Foulkes, Irene. "El costo del discipulado (Hechos 3-4)." *Xilotl* 18:9 (Diciembre 1996), pp. 129-134.

González, Justo L. "A Hispanic Perspective: By the Rivers of Babylon." In *Preaching Justice: Ethnic and Cultural Perspectives*. Edited by Christine Marie Smith. Cleveland: United Church Press, 1998, pp. 80-97.

Gutiérrez, Rolando. "El socorro de Job (Salmo 121 y Job 7)." *Xilotl* 18:9 (Diciembre 1996), pp. 135-39.

Jiménez, Pablo A. "Apuntes bibliográficos para la predicación." *El Educador Cristiano*, Tercera época (Febrero 1990), pp. 22-24.

———. "Aspectos bíblicos del sermón narrativo." *El Evangelio* 54:3 (Julio-Septiembre 1999), pp. 12-13.

————. "Cómo diseñar sermones narrativos." *El Evangelio* 54:2 (Abril-Junio 1999), pp. 12-13.

————. "Cómo planear nuestra predicación." *Apuntes* 21:3 (Otoño 2001), pp. 98-108.

————. "Cómo preparar sermones bíblicos." *El Evangelio* 53:4 (October-December 1998): 28-29.

————. "Cómo preparar un sermón con la Biblia de estudio." *La Biblia en las Américas* 49:5, # 214 (Septiembre-Octubre 1994), pp. 11-12.

————. "¿Dónde nace un sermón?" *El Evangelio* 55:1 (Enero-Marzo 2000), pp. 12-13.

————. "El desafío de la mujer cananea." *La Biblia en las Américas* 49:2, #211 (Marzo-Abril 1994), pp. 13-15.

————. "El modelo del líder." *La Biblia en las Américas* 48:1, # 204 (Enero-Febrero 1993), pp. 9-11.

————. "El sermón de ocasión." *El Evangelio* 54:4 (Octubre-Diciembre 1999), pp. 12-13.

————. "El sermón narrativo." *El Evangelio* 54:1 (Enero-Marzo 1999), pp. 12-13.

————. "Elusive Honor." In *Shaken Foundations: Sermons from America's Pulpits after the Terrorist Attacks.* Edited by David P. Polk. St. Louis: Chalice Press, 2001, pp. 104-9.

————. "Estudio bíblico y hermenéutica: Implicaciones homiléticas." In *Lumbrera a nuestro camino.* Edited by Pablo A. Jiménez. Miami: Editorial Caribe, 1994.

————. "From Text to Sermon with Philippians 1:1-6: A Hispanic Reading." *Apuntes* 17:2 (Verano 1997), pp. 35-40.

————. "In Search of a Hispanic Model of Biblical Interpretation." *Journal of Hispanic / Latino Theology* 3:2 (Noviembre 1995), pp. 44-64.

————. "Laborers of the Vineyard (Matthew 20:1-16): A Hispanic Homiletic Reading." *Journal for Preachers* 21:1 (Adviento 1997), pp. 35-40.

————. "The Laborers of the Vineyard (Matthew 20:1-16): A Hispanic Homiletic Reading." *Academy of Homiletics,* Papers of the 32nd Annual Meeting, 1997.

————. "Los tres pasos." *El Discípulo* 2:2 (Septiembre-Febrero 1994), pp. 215-17.

————. "Nuevos horizontes en la predicación." En *Púlpito cristiano y justicia social.* Editado por Daniel R. Rodríguez and Rodolfo Espinosa. México: Publicaciones El Faro, 1994.

————. "¿Qué es la predicación bíblica?" *El Educador Cristiano,* Tercera época (Febrero 1990), pp. 4-7.

————. "Predicadores, profetas y sacerdotes." *La Biblia en las Américas* 53 #236 (#4 1998), pp. 23-25.

————. "Predicación y Postmodernidad: Dos aportes a la discusión." *Apuntes* 19:1 (Primavera 1999), pp. 3-7.

————. "Religión electrónica y predicación protestante." *Pasos,* Segunda época, 13 (Septiembre 1987), pp. 10-13.

―――. "Reseña: Comunicación y proclamación del evangelio hacia el siglo XXI." *Vida y Pensamiento* 6:2 (1986), pp. 66-67.

―――. "Reseña: El trípode homilético: Una guía para predicadores laicos por Carlos Emilio Ham." *Apuntes* 21:3 (Fall 2001): 117-18.

―――. "Reseña: Siervo de la palabra: Manual de homilética por Christophe Zenses." *Vida y Pensamiento* 18:1 (1998): 102-04.

―――. "Reseña: Siervo de la palabra: Manual de homilética por Christophe Zenses." *Apuntes* 18:3 (Otoño 1998): 93-94.

―――. "Reseña: Teoría y práctica de la predicación por Cecilio Arrastía." *Apuntes* 14.1 (Primavera 1994), pp. 29-31.

―――. "Teaching Hispanics Old Testament Interpretation: A Bibliographical Essay." *Academy of Homiletics*, Papers of the 33nd Annual Meeting, 1998.

―――. "Teaching Homiletics to Hispanic Students: A Bibliographical Essay." *Academy of Homiletics*, Papers of the 35th Meeting (2000): 149-54.

Kater, John L., S.V. "Homiletics and Preaching in Latin America" in *Concise Encyclopedia of Preaching*. Edited by William M. Willimon and Richard Lischer. (Louisville: Westminster/John Knox Press, 1995), pp. 241-43.

Kidner, Derek. "Predicando el Antiguo Testamento." *Aletheia* 9 (1/1996), pp. 21-34.

Loubriel, Virginia. "La predicación y el ministerio educativo de la iglesia." *El Educador Cristiano*, Tercera época (Febrero 1990), pp. 8-12.

Machado, Daisy. "El cántico de María." *Journal for Preachers* 21:1 (Adviento 1997), pp. 12-15.

Mahler, Kenneth. "Escucha esta palabra: Así dice el Señor: La predicación profética en nuestros tiempos." *Xilotl* 18:9 (Diciembre 1996), pp. 37-50.

Nahlis, Michéle. "Gozos y peligros de la predicación." *Xilotl* 18:9 (Diciembre 1996), pp. 83-98.

Pixley, Jorge V. "El predicador como profeta de Dios ante su pueblo: El modelo de Jeremías." *Xilotl* 18:9 (Diciembre 1996), pp. 17-36.

Resto, Maritza. "El lugar de la predicación en el quehacer pastoral." *El Educador Cristiano*, Tercera época (Febrero 1990), pp. 13-15.

Robleto, Adolfo. "He aquí, yo hago nuevas todas las cosas (Apocalipsis 21:5)." *Xilotl* 18:9 (Diciembre 1996), pp. 99-109.

Rosa, Moisés. "La predicación y la realidad puertorriqueña." *El Educador Cristiano*, Tercera época (Febrero 1990), pp. 19-21.

Valerio, Ivette. "La parábola del juez y la viuda (Lucas 18.1-9)." *Xilotl* 18:9 (Diciembre 1996), pp. 141-46.

Van Seters, Arthur. "Una hermenéutica social hacia una revolución en la predicación." *Vida y Pensamiento* 2:1 (Enero-Junio 1982), pp. 42-52.

Velásquez, Roger. "Una pastoral de nuestro tiempo." *Xilotl* 18:9 (Diciembre 1996), pp. 111-28.

Vilanova, Evangelista. "El servicio de promover la fe." *Xilotl* 18:9 (Diciembre 1996), pp. 9-15.

Books

A. Surveys

Arrastía, Cecilio. *Teoría y práctica de la predicación*. Miami: Caribe, 1978.

Broadus, John. *Tratado sobre la predicación*. El Paso: Casa Bautista de Publicaciones, 1925.

Costas, Orlando E. *Comunicación por medio de la predicación*. San José: Caribe, 1973.

Crane, James D. *El sermón eficaz*. El Paso: Casa Bautista de Publicaciones, 1961.

———. *Manual para predicadores laicos*. El Paso: Casa Bautista de Publicaciones, 1966.

Jiménez, Pablo A. *Principios de predicación*. Nashville: Abingdon Press, 2003.

Mergal, Angel M. *El arte cristiano de la predicación*. El Paso: CUPSA, 1951.

Mottesi, Osvaldo. *Predicación y misión: Una perspectiva pastoral*. Miami: Logoi, 1989.

Rodríguez, Rafael A. *Homilética simplificada*. San Juan: Katallage, 1983.

Rostagno, Bruno. *La fe nace por el oír: Guía para la predicación*. Buenos Aires: La Aurora, 1989.

Vila, Samuel. *Homilética*. Terrassa (Barcelona): CLIE, 1978.

Zenses, Christophe. *Siervo de la palabra: Manual de predicación*. Manual EDU-CAB. Buenos Aires: ISEDET, 1997.

B. Theology and Preaching

Barth, Karl. *La proclamación del evangelio*. Salamanca: Sígueme, 1969.

Boff, Leonardo. *Teología desde el lugar del pobre*. Santander: Sal Terrae, 1986.

Costas, Orlando E., editor. *Predicación evangélica y teología hispana*. Miami: Editorial Caribe/San Diego: Editorial Las Américas, 1982.

Grasso, Doménico. *Teología de la predicación: El ministerio de la palabra*. Salamanca: Ediciones Sígueme, 1969.

Maldonado, Luis. *El menester de la predicación*. Salamanca: Ediciones Sígueme, 1972.

Ratzinger, Joseph. *Palabra en la Iglesia*. Salamanca: Ediciones Sígueme, 1976.

C. Collections of Essays

Arrastía, Cecilio. *La predicación, el predicador y la iglesia*. Edited by Plutarco Bonilla. San José: CELEP, 1983.

Carty, Marjorie T. and James W. Jr., editors. *Comunicación y proclamación del evangelio hacia el siglo XXI*. México: CUPSA, 1984.

Castro, Emilio. *Pastores del pueblo de Dios en América Latina*. Buenos Aires: La Aurora, 1973.

Rodríguez, Daniel, y Rodolfo y Espinosa, editors. *Púlpito cristiano y justicia social*. México: El Faro, 1994.

D. Collections of Sermons

Arrastía, Cecilio. *A pesar de todo . . . Dios sigue siendo amor*. Miami: Editorial Caribe, 1994.

———. *Itinerario de la pasión: Meditaciones para la Semana Santa*. El Paso: Casa Bautista de Publicaciones, 1978.

———. *Jesucristo, Señor del Pánico: Antología de Predicaciones*. Miami: UNILIT, 1985.

Barth, Karl. *Al servicio de la palabra*. Salamanca: Edicines Sigueme, 1985.

Cardona, José A. *Semana Mayor*. San Juan: Librería La Reforma, San Juan, 1977.

Gutiérrez, Angel Luis, editor. *Voces del púlpito hispano*. Valley Forge: Judson Press, 1989.

Pagán, Samuel. *Púlpito, teología y esperanza*. Miami: Caribe, 1988.

Rad, Gerhard von. *Sermones*. Salamanca: Ediciones Sígueme, 1975.

Ropero, Alfonso. *Lo mejor de San Juan Crisóstomo*. Terrassa (Barcelona): CLIE, 2002.

E. Biblical Preaching

Blackwood, Andrew W. *La preparación de sermones bíblicos*. El Paso: Casa Bautista de Publicaciones, 1953.

Freeman, Harold. *Nuevas alternativas en la predicación bíblica*. El Paso: Casa Bautista de Publicaciones, 1990.

Jiménez, Pablo A., editor. *Lumbrera a nuestro camino*. Miami: Editorial Caribe, 1994.

Kempff, Gerardo, Juan Bernt, and Roberto Huebner. *Predicando a Cristo: Comentarios a las lecturas bíblicas para cada domingo*. St. Louis: Editorial Concordia, 2003.

MacCarthur, John Jr., editor. *Predicación expositiva: Cómo balancear la ciencia y el arte de la exposición bíblica*. Nashville: Editorial Caribe, 1996.

Perry, Lloyd M. *Predicación bíblica para el mundo actual*. Miami: Vida, 1986.

Santander Franco, José. *Introducción a la predicación bíblica*. Grand Rapids, Mich.: Libros Desafío, 1991.

Turnbull, Rodolfo G., editor. *Diccionario de la teología práctica: Homilética*. Grand Rapids, Mich.: TELL, 1976.

F. Specialized Books

Aldazabal, José. *El arte de la homilía*. Barcelona: Centre de Pastoral Litúrgica, 1979.

Broadus, John A. *Historia de la predicación: Discursos.* El Paso: Casa Bautista de Publicaciones, sin fecha.
CELAM. *La homilía: ¿Qué es? ¿Cómo se prepara? ¿Cómo se presenta?* Bogotá: Departamento de Liturgia del CELAM, 1981.
Comisión Episcopal de Liturgia. *Partir el pan de la palabra.* Madrid: Promoción Popular Cristiana, 1990.
Costas, Orlando E. *Introducción a la comunicación.* San José: Sebila, 1976.
Garvie, Alfredo Ernesto. *Historia de la predicación cristiana.* Terrassa (Barcelona): CLIE, 1987.
Howe, Reuel L. *El milagro del diálogo.* San José: Celadec, sin fecha.
Limardo, Miguel. *Ventanas abiertas.* Kansas City: Casa Nazarena, 1969.
Mohana, Jono. *Cómo ser un buen predicador: Teoría y ejercicios para desarrollar elocuencia, voz, expresión corporal, estilo, memoria y contenidos.* Buenos Aires: Lumen, 1995.
Ovando, Jorge. *El sentido profético del predicador.* Miami: Caribe, 1996.
Palau, Luis. *Predicación: Manos a la obra.* Miami: UNILIT, 1995.
Spurgeon, Charles Haddon. *Discursos a mis estudiantes.* El Paso: Casa Bautista de Publicaciones, 1950.
Stott, John. *El cuadro bíblico del predicador.* Terrassa (Barcelona): CLIE, 1975.
———. *Imágenes del predicador en el Nuevo Testamento* (Revised edition of *El cuadro bíblico del predicador*). Buenos Aires: Nueva Creación, 1996.
Vilá, Samuel. *Anécdotas.* Terrassa (Barcelona): CLIE, 1970.

G. Books in English

Davis, Kenneth and Jorge L. Presmanes, editors. *Preaching and Culture in Latino Congregations.* Chicago: Liturgical Training Publications, 2000.
González, Justo L., and Catherine G. González. *Liberation Preaching.* Nashville: Abingdon Press, 1980.
———. *The Liberating Pulpit.* Nashville: Abingdon Press, 1995.

CPSIA information can be obtained at www.ICGtesting.com
Printed in the USA
LVOW071808300812

296719LV00017B/183/P